Practical Godliness

The Ornament of All Religion

Being the Subject of Several Sermons
Upon Titus 2:10

by
Vincent Alsop
Minister of the Gospel

Edited by Dr. Don Kistler

Soli Deo Gloria Publications
. . . for instruction in righteousness . . .

Soli Deo Gloria Publications
A Division of Soli Deo Gloria Ministries
P. O. Box 451, Morgan PA 15064
(412)221-1901/FAX 221-1902
www.SDGbooks.com

*

*

ISBN 1-57358-145-3

*

Library of Congress Cataloging-in-Publication Data

Alsop, Vincent, 1629 or 30-1703.
    Practical godliness : the ornament of all religion : being the
subject of several sermons upon Titus 2:10 / by Vincent Alsop ;
edited by Don Kistler.
        p. cm.
    ISBN 1-57358-145-3 (alk. paper)
1. Bible. N.T. Titus II, 10–Sermons. 2. Christian life–Early works to
1800. 3. Christian life–Biblical teaching. 4. Sermons, English–17th
century. 5. Presbyterian Church-Sermons. I. Kistler, Don. II. Title.
BS2755.54 .A47 2004
252'.03–dc22

                                        2003017484

Contents

Contents

Appendix

To the Reader

To all who love the Lord Jesus Christ in sincerity, especially to those who attend upon His ministry, grace and peace.

Beloved Brethren,

What was once preached to your ears is now presented to your eyes, accompanied with fervent prayers that the God of all grace would powerfully impress it upon your hearts. The importunity of friends is a common apology for publishing some pieces which, if affection had not more prevailed than judgment, might as well never have seen the light. How much of this I might plead to justify or excuse my appearing in print upon this subject many of you know, but I shall willingly waive those reasons. The weight, the worth, and the necessity of the arguments have been my strongest inducements, so they are all I shall offer for my vindication.

The age into which Sovereign providence has cast our lot boasts of much light. I wish that a proportionate measure of holy heat had accompanied that light; that grace, truth, and peace might have been the glory of our times. But here we must bitterly lament that the holy flame of zeal for the concerns of Jesus Christ, that fervent love to all who bear His image in righteousness and true holiness, has degenerated into, or been expelled by, another fire, not kindled from heaven, but (if we may judge the cause by the effects) from a contrary origin. The spirit of envy has almost eaten up holy em-

ulation. And we have disputed so furiously about truth
that we have almost lost the other half of our religion,
charity. The noise of axes and hammers in building the
temple has been as great as once it was in destroying it.
This clamor has drowned the softer whispers of the
spirit of holiness and peace; our speculations about
what is too high for our reach, and our quarrels about
what is too low for our serious regard, have insensibly
worn out practical godliness, and in the mean time religion suffers, its enemies triumph, its few cordial
friends mourn over it, and suffer with it.

The gospel of our blessed Savior, if it might have
been heard, would easily have compromised all our
differences; but it has fared no better with religion
than with that charitable person who, interposing
between two friends engaged with drawn swords, was in
the heat of passionate folly avoided by them both for an
unkind reward of his kindness.

It is much to be feared that this will be the
undeserved fate of whoever shall undertake to reconcile
contending friends, to make them both his bitter
enemies; for in an age of fiery, mistaken zeal, he who is
not scalding hot shall be censured for lukewarm; and
not to be a bigot will be to be reputed not a Christian.

The only expedient I can recommend to you, my
beloved brethren, in this sad case is to maintain innocence in your own souls, peace in your own consciences, to keep close to your duty; and if for endeavors
of love you must be so unhappy as to contract enmity, to
retire with the psalmist to your God (Psalm 109:4) and
give yourselves unto prayer.

But as the holy gospel of God our Savior suffers
unworthily by our divisions and contentions, it suffers

no less by our unsuitable conversations, which yet are but the evil effect of an evil cause, the bitter fruit of that poisonous root. For as when one part of the natural body grows great beyond its proportion, it robs the rest of their due nourishment and growth; such is our deplorable case. We have furnished the head so plentifully with notions that we have starved the members of their proper supplies so that they cannot perform their proper operations. We have laid out so much of our zeal and vigor upon controversies that there's little left to support the necessary things of practical religion—holiness towards God, repentance from dead works, the exercise of good works, and a heavenly conversation.

I bless God from my soul that most of you are of another temper and character; though I cannot deny that the enemy has studied to sow tares among you. And while we slept, his emissaries and instruments have watched to bring in among you some doctrines and practices which would have wounded, if not mortally stabbed, our holy profession. But blessed be the great Superintendent of His church, who faithfully watched over you, and against them, and has prevented and defeated their subtle malice.

It is for the sake of humble, sincere ones principally that I have drawn up and sent forth these papers; who cannot perhaps wield a heavy argument for the cause of Christ and against its opposers, and yet their integrity and uprightness keeps them secure. And the grace of God, on which they humbly and securely depend, enables them to live down all the objections of atheists, deists, and profane persons, by a regular and exemplary conversation.

We read of a philosopher who, when a subtle sophister disputed zealously that there was no such thing as motion in the world, said nothing, but rose up and walked. You may possibly meet with such profane wretches who, with great noise and clamor, would bear you down that there's nothing real, nothing solid in religion; that it is an empty, ineffectual notion, a curious, airy speculation, that has no power upon men's hearts, no command over their lives. Now if you shall meet with this importunate clamor, which is the best argument they have, say nothing, but rise up and walk. Let men see your holy, heavenly conversation, and this will silence all their cavils, and stop the mouths of all their objections, better than you can do by fine force and dint of argument.

And indeed, let us dispute and write what and while we please, nothing will vindicate religion from the reproaches thrown upon it by impudent atheism but the holy walking of those who profess it. And it is a thousand pities that false doctrine should be credited by a severe, morose, and rigid behavior, while truth itself is blemished and brought into contempt by a loose one.

Let me therefore anticipate the following discourse thus far as to assure you that the credit of our holy religion can never be recovered without:

• A more conscientious sanctification of the Lord's Day; all practical religion rises, falls, ebbs, and flows with that. When a generation of men removed the observation of that day from divine institution, and laid it upon the church's tradition or the civil sanction, the repute of it sunk presently, and the observation of it dwindled away to nothing.

• A more constant, fixed worshipping of God in our families. As personal remissness will creep into the family, so will family looseness easily infect the churches. It is in vain to dream that congregations will be holy if families are profane.

This one thing further, brethren, I have to beg of you, or rather of God for you, that you may most zealously and unweariedly pursue the things that make for truth, holiness, and peace, and never to divide those things which God has joined together, and God, even our God, shall give you His blessing. This is the unfeigned desire, and shall ever be the fervent prayer of him who is, and shall endeavor to approve himself to God, to his own conscience, and to yours, to be

The faithful servant of your souls through Christ,

Vincent Alsop
February 25, 1696

1

The Introduction

"That they may adorn the doctrine of God
our Savior in all things." Titus 2:10

The exhortation here given us is of far greater extent than the occasion on which it was given. The occasion was narrow, but the equitable construction is wide. It was given immediately to servants, but it reaches their masters—none so low as to be beneath it, none so high as to be above it. The poorest servant in his humble capacity must demean himself with that fidelity and integrity, so that he may adorn the doctrine of the gospel. The highest prince in his exalted orb must remember that he has a Lord and Master in heaven. In a word, whatever figure any one makes, whatever character he wears, in whatever relation he stands, whatever place he fills, yet he comes within the compass of this command: to walk soberly, righteously, and religiously, so that he may adorn the doctrine of God our Savior in all things.

The Christian religion is a piece of exact symmetry, a face of excellent beauty. 'Tis all glorious within, and its clothing is of wrought gold (Psalm 45:13). But we must take up a most bitter lamentation over it; its harmony has been disordered, its beauty blemished, and much filth thrown in its face, not only by the reproach of declared enemies, but the unsuitable conversations of those who profess it, who value themselves highly upon it, who pretend to have an interest in it, and their highest hopes and expectations from it. In short, it has been wounded in the house of its friends (Zechariah 13:6).

What Plato once said of virtue may be more justly affirmed of the gospel if it could be seen in its native and genuine beauty: it would allure all eyes, ravish all hearts, draw all men's affections, and raise itself a throne in every man's conscience. But here we must acknowledge with grief and shame that either we have gotten such feeble conceptions of it in our own souls, or so miserably misrepresented it to others that we have rendered it cheap and unlovely, and most wretchedly scandalized it before the sons of men.

If therefore there are any who have already heard, or shall hereafter read, this mean, but well-meaning discourse, whose pious souls are grieved that this holy doctrine has been trampled in the mire by unhallowed feet, or whose consciences have been touched, that they themselves have been the cause of, or given occasion to this scandal, unto such is the word of this exhortation sent. My desire is that they would conscientiously endeavor to retrieve the credit, to vindicate the honor and, in the language of the text, to adorn the doctrine of God our Savior in all things.

In the words of our text you will easily observe three things:

1. The great end which God has propounded to us, and which we are to propound to ourselves: that in the whole course of our conversation, we adorn the doctrine of the gospel.

2. The extent of this exhortation: "in all things," which may refer to all the parts of this holy doctrine; to adorn it in all the precepts, all the promises, all the holy examples laid down therein. Or it may refer to all the various relations wherein we stand, the various conditions wherein the providence of God may cast us, that in all these we make it our business to adorn this doctrine, to beautify this blessed gospel.

3. The reason assigned to enforce this exhortation: it is the doctrine of God our Savior, who is God. It is the doctrine of our God who has authority over us; the doctrine of our Savior, who should have the great commanding interest in us, and our greatest concerns are wrapped up in it. It is the doctrine of a Savior, and it is a saving doctrine, and all the reproach thrown upon this doctrine falls upon Christ. What falls upon Christ falls upon God; and whatever reproach flies so high as God will certainly fall down again with an overwhelming vengeance upon the head of him who throws it.

There is little that will need explication; to clear our way to the doctrine, only two words may deserve some consideration.

"Doctrine" (*didaskalia* or *didache*). These two words denote matter of faith, what we are to believe, or matter of practice, wherein we are to obey. Thus where the apostle, among the other characters of a bishop, requires that he be able by sound doctrine to exhort (Titus 1:9), Occumenius thus glosses it, "Sound doctrine is that which teaches orthodoxy, and a regular conversation." It is that which makes a sound head, in opposition to heresy, and a sound heart in opposition to hypocrisy—and both these will produce sound conduct.

A second word which I will touch upon is "adorn." The adorning commanded is not by painting religion, or adding any artificial color to the face of it; it is not by superinducing any varnish above its natural complexion, for religion needs none of our over-officious skill to deck and trim it up after the newest mode, or to recommend it to the wanton affections of men with a meretricious dress, for gold needs no gilding. But the way of adorning here enjoined is by rubbing off the rust, wiping off the dust, and washing off the dirt, which by the injury of time it has contracted, or by the reproach of enemies it has suffered. The word means that we restore it to its primitive luster, its original simplicity, by walking according to the commands, answering the demands, living up to its ends, and expressing the true native, real glory of it in a suitable conversation.

DOCTRINE: It ought to be the conscientious care of all who profess the gospel of Christ to adorn the doctrine of that gospel in all things.

The apostle lays so great a weight upon this duty, as if it were the one thing, the only thing necessary (Philippians 1:27): "Only let your conversation be as it becometh the gospel of Christ." And there are two subservient duties which will much contribute to this great design. The first is stability, steadfastness in the faith, that you stand fast in the Spirit. The other is a holy zeal, that you strive together for the faith of the gospel. Stand fast without wavering; be zealous without cooling; and let your interest and the name and glory of your Redeemer be much upon your hearts in both of these matters.

Whatever can be said upon this subject is compendiously summed up by the same apostle in Philippians 4:8–9, which I will give you a brief paraphrase upon, and then proceed: "Finally brethren, whatsoever things are true, whatsoever things are honest, whatsoever things are just, whatsoever things are pure, whatsoever things are lovely, whatsoever things are of good report; if there be any virtue, if there be any praise, think on these things. Those things which ye have both learned, and received, and heard, and seen in me, do, and the God of peace shall be with you."

Think on these things, and do them. Digest the matter well in your thoughts; concoct it thoroughly in your hearts, and then reduce all to practice. It is not speculation but action, that must recover the reputation of religion. And the particulars wherein you must be active and zealous are such as these:

• "Whatsoever things are true." Let the power of truth in the heart evidence itself in the life; and let the grace of God in the inward parts shine through the body in all suitable demeanor. It is Theodoret's gloss upon 1 Timothy 3:2 that the apostle would have a bishop to be a man who is so comely in his discourses, in his habit, in his looks and gestures, that the complexion of his soul may shine through the case of his body.

• "Whatsoever things are honest." We are to be grave, yet not morose; serious, yet not austere; reserved without affectation, so that, as the end of our conversation is a matter of the greatest importance, and the rule of our lives of equal concern, the mien and air of our behavior may bear some good conformity to them both.

• "Whatsoever things are just." As we must be holy towards God, so must we also be just towards all men;

for righteousness is evangelism made visible. It is the preaching of a gospel which men understand. Our religion teaches us to give to God and man what is their due, and all the world will conclude that, if we defraud them, we would, if it were in our power, cheat our God too. Nor can we ever confute those suspicions which men will easily entertain of our hypocrisy but by an exact and punctual discharge of all those offices of justice which we owe them.

• "Whatsoever things are pure." We are to be chaste, modest, pure, and clean. Our discourses are not to savor of filthiness; our behavior must not smell rank of inward turpitude; we must not allow the flesh to mingle itself with our courses or discourses, but we must see that in all things our speech is seasoned with salt, administering grace to the hearers (Ephesians 4:29). It is a dirty world we walk in; he who will walk clean must pick and choose his way with great care and conscience.

• "Whatsoever things are lovely." Let a spirit of candor and holy ingenuity breathe in all our actions so that we do not frighten men from religion by a sour, disobliging conduct. There is a median (could we hit it) between a base, creeping, fawning prostitution of ourselves to the lusts of men, and a haughty, surly arrogance which will not stoop or bend to the benefit of men; and this mean is that greatness of humility which would persuade the prejudiced world to entertain more tolerable thoughts of God's holy ways, and perhaps in time to try and practice them.

• "Whatsoever things are of good report." We are to decline those practices which carry an appearance of evil with really good men. Now, says the apostle, if there is any virtue: if ever your religion had any commanding interest in you, or has had any sanctifying power upon you; and if there be any praise: if you expect the acceptance and approbation of God, or the moderate commendation of good men—then think upon and do these things. And, for your encouragement, the God of peace shall be with you.

In managing this doctrine, I propose to show:

What adorning the doctrine of the gospel presupposes.

What it is to adorn the doctrine of the gospel in all things.

What the particulars of the doctrine are which we must adorn, and how it may be adorned in each of these particulars.

I will lay down the arguments which ought to prevail with us herein. And last, I will endeavor to apply the whole discourse and reduce it to practice.

2

What This Exhortation Presupposes

There was something more than ordinary in the matter that caused the apostle to so earnestly and frequently press this point. Some injury had been offered from which it needed to be vindicated; something amiss in their conversation needed reformation. And we have cause to fear that the case is our own. Some notable affront has been put upon the gospel, some indignity offered to the profession or religion, which will render our present discourse too pertinent. That which is presupposed may be reduced to these headings:

1. That we are so earnestly urged to adorn the doctrine of our God and Savior presupposes that, as it came first out of the hands of Christ, it was altogether lovely; representing the sweetness and expressing the holiness of Him who gave it forth.

One eminent beauty of the doctrine is that those truths which soar the highest in speculation in their design and tendency aim at a holy, practical conversation; those doctrines which in theory reach the highest heavens in their scope stoop down to the earth. It was said of Socrates that he was the first who brought philosophy down from the clouds and made it a useful thing to human life. It was greater which was said of our own Mr. Perkins: "He was the first who among us reduced doctrine to application, and speculation to practice." However that may be, most certain it is that every truth, doctrine, and proposition in the gospel aims at subduing sin in the heart, and, bringing the heart to God, seeks to make us better rather than wiser. The design of the Scripture is not to amuse and puzzle us, but to reform and sanctify us; not to confound our heads, but to conform our hearts and reform our lives to the holiness of its principles; not to make us lose our wits, but to save our souls. But the truth of this will most clearly appear in some instances.

The doctrine of God's electing some out of the mass of mankind, from all eternity, unto eternal life is a doctrine which swallows up our reasons, and we are lost in the depth of it. Here indeed faith will swim, but naked reason, unassisted by revelation, will certainly sink and drown in that vast abyss; for who is he who, standing upon the shore of that unfathomable gulf, will not cry out with the apostle in Romans 11:33, "Oh, the depth of the riches both of the wisdom and knowledge of God! How unsearchable are His judgments, and His ways past finding out!" And yet, when this sublime doctrine shall produce its effects in calling home souls to God, it comes clothed with visible grace, approves itself to our experience, and terminates in practical godliness. Ephesians 1:4: "According as He hath chosen us in Him before the foundation of the world; that we should be holy, and without blame before Him in love." Think of the the sun, whose glory we can neither safely behold nor gaze upon in its meridian luster without endangering our eyes; yet we can comfortably view it by reflection. So that doctrine which would strike us blind in its direct and immediate prospect administers a sweet and sensible consolation when it comes to take hold upon the heart in effectual calling.

Those curious speculations which men have spun out of their own brains, and woven in subtle webs, as the spider her nets out of her own bowels, are but elaborate nothings, refined trifles. We may know them and be never the better; we may be ignorant of them and never be the worse. Only gospel doctrines have this singular excellency, that they bear hard upon the corruption of the heart to mortify it, upon pride to abase it, and press vigorously upon the conscience to purify and pacify it. They are therefore called "wholesome words," even the words of our Lord Jesus Christ, and the "doctrine which is according to godliness" (1 Timothy 6:3). They are wholesome in themselves and healing to the soul; such as, being taken into the heart, purge out the corruption of depraved nature, and in a word, it's a doctrine whose every line is drawn by the straight rule of holiness, and centers in that one point of godliness.

The doctrine of redemption is another great instance of this truth. What is more amazing than that God should send and give His Son, and that the Son should give and offer up Himself to redeem lost (self-lost) sinners; to redeem them by price paid to God out of the hand of justice; to redeem them by power out of the hand of the devil. This would lead us back to the covenant of redemption between the eternal Father and the eternal Son, when the council of peace was between them both (Zechariah 6:13). But here we may lose ourselves, and perhaps not find out God, till we relieve ourselves by such Scriptures as Titus 2:14: "He gave Himself for us to redeem us from all iniquity, and purify unto Himself a peculiar people zealous of good works." He not only redeems us from hell, but sin; not only to purchase, but to purify us to Himself; not only to deliver us from the future, but from this present evil world (Galatians 1:4); not only to rescue us out of the devil's power, but out of our own—and thus this doctrine terminates in godliness, in good works, for so the apostle concludes his discourse: "that He might purify unto Himself a peculiar people, zealous of good works."

Another peculiar glory of the doctrine of the gospel is that it never more directly designs the advancement of a sinner than when it abases him most and lays him lowest; it suits indeed the sinner's misery, but always crosses his lust; it empties the creature when it designs to fill him, and humbles the proud worm so that it may exalt it. The gospel breaks first, and then binds up; wounds that it may heal, and condemns that it may justify. It will make the sinner plead guilty before he is absolved. It strips him naked before it clothes him, and makes him know, see, and feel himself to be the most beggarly wretch in the world before it discovers the unsearchable riches of Christ. In a word, it will convince us all that we are the most miserable, undone, lost things ere it saves us.

And in this point the apostle has fully satisfied us that the method of the infinitely wise God issues in this: "that no flesh might glory in His presence, but he that glorieth, let him glory in the Lord" (1 Corinthians 1:29, 31).

In election, God had no respect to faith, works, or the right use of free will foreseen, that no flesh might glory in His presence. The same method He takes in justifying a sinner: "that no flesh might glory in His presence." So Romans 3:27: "Where is boasting then? It is excluded! By what law? Of works? Nay, but by the law of faith."

There are two things upon which the haughty creature would value itself: its own righteousness and its own strength. And we may add a third, its own wisdom. Upon these especially the proud worm lifts up its crest on high; the gracious God has provided in His covenant that the sinner shall have righteousness, shall have strength, shall have wisdom—but not his own, but God's.

Righteousness is one of the strongholds wherein the proud flesh fortifies itself, and goes about to establish its own righteousness (Romans 10:3). And this stronghold God will dismantle, and level it with the ground, before He builds the house upon the impregnable rock of His own righteousness, that is, the righteousness of Christ. Conviction of sin and comparing ourselves with the holy perfect law of God will thoroughly effect this, and then the sinner stands upon other terms with God and his own conscience. You shall hear this stately, proud creature speaking in another language when he comes to be distressed about his sin. Micah 6:6: "Wherewithal shall I come before the Lord, and bow myself before the most high God?"

What perplexity is there between the necessity of coming and the hazard of coming? "I must come before the Lord either to be justified or judged. I must come before Him at both the footstool and the throne; but wherewithal to come, or what to bring that I may be accepted in His sight, I do not find. My own unrighteousness I see now to be abominable, and my own righteousness I am convinced is not justifiable. Wherewithal then shall I come?" In this distress, the gospel reveals Christ and His righteousness. And when the sinner accepts, receives, lays hold of, and rests upon it, it has encouragement to say, as Isaiah 45:24–25, "In the Lord have I righteousness; in the Lord shall all the seed of Jacob be justified, and shall glory." Here then shines out the glory of the gospel doctrine; it never designs a more perfect cure than when it makes the sinner sick at heart. Thus the Spirit's method is, first, to convince of sin, and then of righteousness (John 16:8), of sin that the sinner may be abased and made willing to accept a pardon upon Christ's terms, and of righteousness that the wounded soul may not die of its wounds; for thus was the brazen serpent lifted up, that they who were mortally stung by the fiery ones might look and live (John 3:14–15).

Another stronghold which man would build upon, and which God will demolish, is man's own strength. It is unaccountable that man should thus idolize his own often-baffled, often-soiled strength, which was never yet able to make him stand against his own corruptions, the world's allurements, or the assaults and wiles of the Tempter. It is the grace of God alone that must take us off our own foundation and place us upon a stronger one, and teach us how to be strong in the Lord and in the power of His might (Ephesians 6:10). And now whereas the late difficulty was, "Wherewithal shall I appear before the Lord?" another difficulty appears; and I find that I can no more appear against the devil in my own strength than I could appear before the Lord in my own righteousness. He is subtle and strong. I am foolish and weak, yet the Gospel has relieved me. Isaiah 45:24: "Surely shall one say, 'In the Lord, have I strength.' "

A third peculiar glory of the doctrine of the gospel is that, as it lays the creature low, it exalts and lifts up

God on high. When a sinner lies prostrate at God's foot, it sees the Lord most gloriously exalted upon His throne (Isaiah 6:1). There's no doctrine that so vilifies man, and none that so much glorifies God. In all other systems which philosophers had framed to themselves, they provided well to advance the creature; they furnished him with a free will, and put him into the hand of his own wisdom to carve himself out a happiness. They made a God of their own moral virtues, and those virtues were at their own disposal, so that upon the matter they were creators of their gods. "That you are happy, you owe to yourself" was one of their highly celebrated maxims. But the doctrine of the gospel clearly gives another scheme of things: man is nothing, knows nothing, can do nothing, cannot think a good thought nor pursue it to any good resolution, nor manage the good, nor beat the evil by his own wisdom of strength. This doctrine teaches us to think meanly of ourselves and highly of God; to look upon ourselves as worms, as moths, as nothing, less than nothing, and worse than nothing. But how honorably it teaches us to think and to speak of God; how reverently to worship Him, how holily to walk before Him; with what confidence to trust Him, with what fervor of soul to love Him, and, in short, to make Him the first and last of all.

The fourth and last peculiar glory of the doctrine of the gospel which I shall name at present is that it never exalts one of the divine attributes to the derogation of another. Here is mercy exalted, but withal justice satisfied; and while the free grace of God is upon the throne, holiness is enthroned with it. God can no more pardon without security to His justice than He can punish with inconsistency to His mercy.

The minds of men are strangely deluded in this matter for, looking only upon mercy, they forget the severity of His justice; and if an imaginary mercy would but answer the ends of their presumptions, they take no further thought what becomes of the essential holiness of God. But infinite wisdom has secured and sweetly adjusted the interests of these two great attributes. Romans 3:26: "That He may be just, and the Justifier of him that believeth in Jesus." God will justify (there's mercy), but He will be just in justifying (there's provision made for His justice). The justice of God is satisfied in Christ. The mercy of God is magnified on the believing sinner. Thus God will not lose His glory, and the believing sinner shall not lose his soul.

There seems to be a difficulty in Exodus 34:6–7, where we read of a God pardoning iniquity, transgression, and sin, and yet a God who will by no means clear the guilty. A perplexing riddle indeed. If God will by no means clear the guilty, how does He pardon transgression? But His justice is as peremptory as His mercy is free. He will no more pardon transgression without due compensation to His justice than He will condemn the sinner who by faith lays hold on that compensation which His wisdom has provided, and His grace offered in the gospel. Here then, mercy and truth are met together, righteousness and peace have kissed each other. And all the attributes of God sweetly embrace and harmoniously agree when the satisfaction of one makes way for the exerting and exercising of the other (Psalm 85:10).

2. That we are so earnestly pressed to adorn the doctrine of God our Savior, presupposes that, however beautiful this doctrine is in itself, it has been miserably

blackened, defaced, defiled, and much dirt thrown in the face of it. This is done in various ways.

First, when—from the doctrine of divine grace, mercy, forbearance, and forgiveness—corrupt heads and rotten hearts draw conclusions of licentiousness; that is, when they interpret grace into presumption, which is evidently to subvert the end and design, to invert the order and whole method of the gospel doctrine. For though the gospel proclaims pardon of all sin to the repenting, it indulges none to the impenitent sinner. He who by sinning presumes to find work for mercy shall find to his cost that he was making work for vengeance. The corruption of depraved nature has discovered itself in many instances; these especially evidence its malignity:

• When men will be evil because God has been good. The design of His goodness, patience, and long-suffering is to lead them to repentance (Romans 2:4). But if this goodness is despised; if because God is long-suffering they will be the longer in sinning; if because mercy is still striving with them, they will outstrive that mercy—they will be convinced that they are treasuring up to themselves wrath against the day of wrath, and the revelation of the righteous judgment of God.

Man will be and do evil that God may be good in pardoning. Such there are who say, as in Romans 3:8, "Let us do evil that good may come; let us sin that grace may abound!" Against this presumption the apostle thunders out a just damnation; and because that they might pretend that this was only the consequence of that doctrine of free grace which he preached, he abhors it as a scandalous report, and that his doctrine abetted no such abominable inference he owns indeed,

Romans 5:20, that where sin abounded, grace did much
more abound. But he denies the consequence, chapter
6:1, that therefore any should continue in sin that
grace might abound.

The Apostle Jude, in verse 4, notes those ungodly
ones who turned the grace of God into lasciviousness.
These things deserve observation: (1) what it was they
thus wretchedly abused. It was the grace of God; not the
work of grace upon their hearts, for that they were
strangers to. They were such as had thrown off all worship of God. But it was the doctrine of grace, which is
indeed sometimes called grace because it is a revelation
of free rich grace offered to the sons of men. (2) Into
what did they turn this grace? Into lasciviousness, or an
unbridled license to commit all manner of iniquity
with greediness. (3) But how could they do this abominable thing! They did it by a metathesis; most wickedly
transposing, inverting, and perverting the order,
method, and design of God and His gospel in everything. And what should have been the strongest argument to withdraw them from sin, they made their great
encouragement to sin, and thus they turned the point
of God's argument upon Himself.

• When men take up a profession and form of religion, but deny the power of it upon their hearts and in
their lives, this is one of the characters of those per-
ilous, those last and worst of days. 2 Timothy 3:5:
"Having a form of godliness, but denying the power
thereof." For the great end of the gospel is to convert
sinners unto God, to subdue them to the authority of
Christ; but these wretches represent it as a weak and in-
efficacious doctrine that has no power nor prevalency
upon their souls. They deny the power of it. There's

nothing more certain than that if men's religion does not drive out their lusts, their lusts will drive away their religion; and yet these will be lovers of their own selves, covetous, boasters, unthankful, unholy, without natural affection, truce-breakers, false accusers, incontinent, fierce, and despisers of them who are good, and yet, which is amazing, they will maintain a form of godliness.

If you ask them, "Do you believe in God the Father Almighty, Maker of heaven and earth?" They will tell you they firmly believe it. Ask them again: "Do you believe in Jesus Christ, His only Son our Lord; that He was conceived by the Holy Ghost, born of the Virgin Mary, that He suffered under Pontius Pilate, was crucified, dead and buried, that He descended into hell?" Ask them all the other articles of the creed. All these they steadfastly believe! But when this doctrine commands subjection of soul to all these truths, that we should live for Him who died for us, and rose again (2 Corinthians 5:15), in this point they desire to be excused; which is an evident affront to the gospel, whose design is to turn them to God from idols, to serve the living and true God (1 Thessalonians 1:9). This evidences that the gospel comes not in word only, but in power, and in the Holy Ghost (verse 5). And so the same apostle, in Romans 6:17, gives thanks to God that they who had once been the servants of sin had obeyed from their heart that form of doctrine which was delivered unto them; or rather, that unto which they had been delivered.

Men may be sound and orthodox in their heads, and yet heterodox and rotten in their hearts. They can afford to lend Christ an ear and give Him a civil hearing, still reserving their lusts to themselves and their hearts for the world. And when the Word demands entrance into, and to have a throne in, their hearts, they deny it the commanding power, and bid it sit below at the footstool, sending away the blessed gospel disappointed and ashamed.

• The gospel has been exceedingly stained when it is entertained for no other end than to serve some base low design of the flesh, and when it is made a slave to some worldly interest. This reproach the Pharisees cast upon their own religion (Matthew 23:14), who, under the covert and color of long prayers, devoured widows' houses. They had a pretense indeed, but it was so thin and transparent that an ordinary eye might see through it, and discover the wicked design at the bottom. Such were they in 1 Timothy 6:5 who supposed gain to be godliness. But most notable was the instance of Simon the Sorcerer in Acts 8:13. This famous hypocrite was baptized, nay, believed and adhered to Philip, and was free of his money too; but all was that he might make his markets of religion, that he might purchase the gift of miracles for himself and his disciples, and so maintain his former reputation that he was some great thing, the very power of God among the deluded people. But all this project was defeated and blown away with one breath from St. Peter's mouth: "Thy money perish with thee."

We have a generation of men in our age, descended from this Simon, who have driven a mighty gainful trade by the gospel; who buy or sell the superintendency of souls; whose money and, we may justly fear, their souls too, and those of their flocks, perish together. These are a horrid scandal to religion, not seeking Christ, but themselves; not feeding the flock, but their own pride and ambition. When the Great Shepherd shall appear, they must be compelled to stand before His presence, but will not dare to lift up their faces with a holy and humble confidence, and shall receive a just recompense of reward.

• A fourth thing that has blemished the doctrine of the gospel is those swarms of damnable doctrines which have been poured out upon the world; of these the apostle in 2 Peter 2:1–2 has prophesied: "There shall be false teachers who privily shall bring in damnable heresies, even denying the Lord that bought them; and bring upon themselves swift destruction. And many shall follow their pernicious ways, by reason of whom the way of truth shall be evil spoken of." That they shall bring upon themselves swift destruction is very sad (that they have deserved), but that the way of truth should be evil spoken of (which has not deserved it) is most deplorable.

3. The third and last thing supposed in the apostle's exhortation is, that every one of us, in our respective places and stations, engage as far as in us lies to restore religion to its primitive luster and splendor, and so to retrieve the reputation of it; to adorn it in all things. In order to this blessed end, I will only at present offer a few things:

Would we recover the original beauty of the doctrine of the gospel? Then we must so walk, so act, and so live as those who believe invisible things to be the greatest realities.

We must walk without breach of that charity which we owe to all men, or pretending to search the heart; we see that many walk as if all their hopes were terminated by their eyes, and that they believe in no other world or reward than what is within the reach of sense.

But this was the glory of the Apostle Paul in 2 Corinthians 4:18, that he looked not at the things that were seen, but at the things not seen. His main scope and hope was in invisible things; an invisible God and an invisible world had such an influence upon his soul that he was borne up under all present pressures; he could glory in all his present tribulations upon the hope of a future recompense. This was what made Moses endure, as seeing Him who was invisible (Hebrews 11:27). And if we search into the reason of this otherwise unaccountable resolution, we have it in Hebrews 11:1: "Faith is the substance of things hoped for, the evidence of things not seen." If faith can render the future world present; if it can represent the unseen world to the eye; if it can bring down heaven and lay it with all its glory before us—it will teach us to live at another rate than we can possibly do upon the proposal of all things to our sense. This will teach us to wait, and to possess our souls in patience while we wait for those things which Christ has promised to them who love Him, and from love obey Him. Romans 8:25: "If we hope for that we see not, then do we with patience wait for it." This was what taught the primitive Christians to rejoice. 1 Peter 1:8: "Whom having not seen, ye love; in whom, though now ye see Him not, yet believing ye rejoice with joy unspeakable and full of glory."

Convince the world that you can trust your God upon His naked word; who will believe your religion has any thing solid and substantial in it if you cannot depend on the promise of Him whom you say you have chosen and taken for your God. We see it evidently, they

who have chosen the world for their portion can trust
its promises and take its word for good payment. What
a reproach then will it be to those who have a better
God, but a worse faith than they who have a worse God?

Let all men therefore see that you dare follow your
God on the credit of His truth; that you can trust Him
to reimburse whatever you shall lay out for His name, or
lose for His sake. Compel men to acknowledge that you
dare avow your consciences against all the damage you
can possibly sustain for it or from it; convince an unbelieving generation that there are those who know their
God so well that they can trust Him, and though you
apprehend you may probably lose something for Him,
yet you shall lose nothing by Him.

Glorious was the faith of Abraham (Hebrews 11:9),
who sojourned in the land of promise as in a strange
country because he could confidently and comfortably
look for a city that had foundations, whose builder and
maker was God (verse 10). Such was the faith of Moses
(verse 25), who "chose rather to suffer affliction with
the people of God than to enjoy the pleasures of sin for
a season; esteeming the reproach of Christ greater
riches than the treasures of Egypt, for he had respect
unto the recompense of reward." In these heroic act-
ings of faith we cannot but observe, first, the different
value that he put upon things; second, the choice he
made in pursuing that evaluation.

First, let us consider his estimate of things. Moses
esteemed the reproach of Christ greater treasures than
the riches of Egypt. The two things put into the opposite scales are the reproach of Christ in the one, and
the treasures of Egypt in the other. And what man looking on these with an eye of sense would not esteem the

treasures of Egypt preferable to reproach and scorn? But there was something that turned the scale in his judgment, something that gave him a holy bias, that he judged the worst thing in religion better than the best thing in Egypt. The best thing that Egypt could boast of or court him with was its treasures; the worst thing religion could affright him with was reproach, especially if it goes so high as an ignominious death. And yet he esteemed the reproach of Christ greater riches than the treasures of Egypt because he kept his eye fast fixed upon the recompense of reward.

Second, let us not wonder if this was the value and estimate he made of things. He chose rather to suffer affliction with the people of God than to enjoy the pleasures of sin for a season. Two things are set before him, and upon his good or evil choice depended life or death, affliction or pleasure. And is this a measuring cast? Or can anyone be long in suspense which to choose? Affliction is evil, pleasure is good. True, but those afflictions were to be borne with the Church of God, in which he might be assured of God's gracious presence, His powerful protection, His seasonable grace to help in time of need. As for the pleasures, they were polluting and perishing pleasures which would leave a sting in the conscience to embitter the remembrance of them; and therefore his judgment swayed and determined his choice that way.

This, and nothing without this, will convince men that you take the promises for true, that these shall be responsible to your faith; that God shall be responsible for His promises, and that His truth, His faithfulness and omnipotence shall be responsible for God.

Third, let this one thing more be apparent, that you

are under a law to God; that the preceptive part of the Word has taken as strong hold upon your hearts as your faith has taken on the promissory part. All the world will be satisfied that you are in good earnest with religion, when you live in the practice of the most flesh-displeasing duties; that you can deny the most profitable temptation to sin, and that you walk as those who firmly believe your religion will bear its own charges. The power of the Word restraining us from the most gainful sin, and constraining us to the most chargeable duty, will be a most pregnant proof that God is with us, and religion in us of a truth.

But let this much suffice for the first general inquiry: what this exhortation to adorn the doctrine of our God and Savior presupposes.

3

What This Exhortation Implies

What does it imply to adorn the doctrine of the gospel in all things? The answer lies in many particulars.

First, it implies that the doctrine of the gospel must be adorned in civil as well as sacred affairs. It is not enough that we demean ourselves decently and reverently in acts of immediate worship; we must walk in the same fear of God, under the same holy awe, in our secular business. Religion must command even our recreations, our diversions, our converses, and our particular callings. As carnal earthly hearts will carnalize their religious performances, so will spiritual minds spiritualize their common employments. It's far short of the whole duty of man. We sanctify the Lord's Day, and we must sanctify our own. God has indeed graciously indulged us six days in the week to labor in, but not one of those days, nor one moment in any of those hours, wherein we may do the work of the devil and the flesh.

If ever we will pretend to credit our religion, we must evidence holiness in the shop as well as in the church—in our own houses as well as in the Lord's. We must be holy in trading as well as praying; we must sanctify the name of God at our own tables as well as at the Lord's Table. 1 Corinthians 10:31: "Whether therefore ye eat or drink, or whatsoever ye do, do all to the glory of God." 1 Peter 1:15: "As He that hath called you is holy, so be ye holy in all manner of conversation," literally, "in all the windings and turnings of your lives." There's nothing lawful, though never so remote from heaven, but may be laid in a right line and due subordination to it; and when we cannot actually intend our ultimate end, yet must we virtually refer all unto it. What has reproached religion is that what warmth we get in the worship of God, we presently lose, and grow lukewarm, perhaps stone-cold, when we depart from it. And thus, whatever we build up at the church in one day, we are plucking down all the week after.

We must adorn the doctrine of God our Savior in all things, in second table duties as well as those of the first. The same God who sees and observes the temper of our hearts in dealing with himself observes it also in our treatings and dealings with men. Would we approve our sincerity before an all-seeing God? Then approve it also in our treatings, conversings, and transactings with men.

There are some excellent first table Christians who will not swear lightly, nor take God's holy name into their mouths profanely, who seem to make conscience of the Lord's Day; who are severe in regulating the worship of God by His Word. And yet, if common fame may be credited, they are under no such severe bonds of conscience in their covenants, contracts, and engagements with their brethren. But the doctrine of the gospel should have taught them another lesson. Titus 2:12 teaches us to carry it righteously towards our neighbor, soberly towards ourselves, and godly towards our God. What a rare pattern was David in Psalm 101:2: "I will behave myself wisely in a perfect way. I will walk

in the midst of my house with a perfect heart." David
wished to be a holy king upon the throne, a holy judge
upon the bench, a holy general in the field, holy in the
city, and holy in the country; for a perfect heart had
taught him to walk wisely in a perfect way.

If therefore we design to vindicate the glory of religion, none must go beyond, overreach, or defraud his
brother (1 Thessalonians 4:6). Our covenants must be
kept, though we suffer by it (Psalm 15:4). Truth must be
spoken to, and kept with our neighbor, and that
neighbor must be every one who partakes with us of a
human nature.

"In all things" means in holy works as well as holy
words. It is not well-saying, but well-doing that must
wipe off the reproach that has been thrown upon our
holy profession. 1 Peter 2:15: "So is the will of God that
by well-doing, ye put to silence the ignorance of foolish
men." Foolish men will be lavish with their tongues;
they will reproach religion and the religious; and this
evil speaking is the effect of their ignorance. But the
question is, how shall we silence them and stop their
mouths for the future? This the apostle resolves as the
direction of God Himself: it is by well-doing. Words are
cheap; works are chargeable, and will cost us more to
perform them.

It is a mortal stab that is given to religion, when the
professors of it talk as high as heaven and yet walk as
low as this dirty earth; when our notions and professions seem too high for this world, and yet too low for
the next. Words without works are a language which
men do not understand; we speak to them in an un-
known tongue. But to be beneficent, charitable, to do
them good, to relieve the distressed, to deliver the

oppressed, and to make peace among contending neighbors, this is a dialect which is vernacular to all the world.

Had we judged a Pharisee by the ear and not by the eye, he would have been the most excellent saint on earth; but our Savior notes them for this in Matthew 23:3: "They say, and do not." Nay our blessed Savior rebukes His own disciples upon this very account in Luke 6:46: "Why call ye Me, 'Lord, Lord,' and do not the things that I say?"

Let that therefore be ours which was the motto of a great man in his time: "Let men see as well as hear us, that our light may so shine before men that they, seeing our good works, may glorify our Father which is in heaven" (Matthew 5:16).

"In all things" means in passive obedience as well as active, in suffering according to the will of God as well as acting in obedience to it. It is a very poor religion that is not worth suffering for. We must expect otherwise no better language than this; "Surely if these professors really believed their God to be faithful and true, they would trust Him. If they believed the recompense of reward, they would venture their all upon it. If they believed their God able to repay them, to reimburse them in what they should lay out and lose for His sake, they would generously forsake all at the call and for the cause of their God."

Sufferings have ever been the test, the ordeal, by which Christ has proved His disciples. In Mark 10:17–18, a young man came running to Christ, as if in great haste for heaven. And that he might justify his obedience, which he hoped would justify him, he avouched to Christ that He had kept all the commandments from his youth. He began early, continued long, and promised to persevere to the end. I confess I suspect he either lied against his conscience or else had a very bad one; and he had been more hopeful if from a sound conviction he had bitterly cried out, "All these commandments I have broken from my youth." But be it so, Christ was willing to try the truth of his active obedience by his passive obedience, and so put him upon this trial: "Go and sell all that thou hast and give to the poor, and thou shalt have treasure in heaven." This was a pinching word indeed! The neck-verse for a hypocrite! I think I see his courage cool, his countenance change and grow pale; amazement and confusion were in his looks; he turned about and went away sorrowful, for he had great possessions.

Upon no lower terms than these must we hope to recover the glory departed from our profession: when we can cast all at Christ's feet, resign all into His hands, and, whether He gives or takes, say with holy Job (Job 1:21), "The Lord giveth, and the Lord hath taken away; blessed be the name of the Lord."

Let us therefore set before our faith, and imitate the father of the faithful (Genesis 22), who, when called of God to offer up his son, his only son, his well-beloved son, the son of the promise—and that in a way which seemed to contravene the law of nature, the positive law of God—yet did not dispute, did not delay, but gave clear demonstration that he had nothing too dear for his God.

"In all things" means whether in a more narrow and private, or in a more enlarged and public capacity. The heavenly orbs are of different diameters, yet they move regularly according to the laws imposed upon them by their Creator. The stars are of differing luster and glory, and yet they shine, and do not begrudge their influences to this lower ungrateful world, which returns them nothing but fogs and mists to obscure their light and beauty. God has placed us all in spheres of different circumferences; however small they are, let our motion be regular and orderly. He has filled us with various degrees of grace and gifts; let us lay out all faithfully. There are various talents with which our Sovereign Lord has entrusted us as to kind or number. 1 Corinthians 12:11: "Wrought by that one, and the same Spirit, dividing to every one severally as He will."

If then our talents be few, let us be faithful in using them and diligent in applying them. The unprofitable servant of Matthew 25 was not condemned because he had but one talent, but because he hid it in a napkin. He who has but a little spot of ground may cultivate it, and show that diligence in improving it, so that it may reward his labor with a blessing.

Since I considered that passage in the history of Absalom (2 Samuel 15:4: "Oh, that I were made judge in the land, that every one that has any suit or cause might come unto me, and I would do him justice"), it has taught me never to be ambitious of great things without more grace to manage them. But we are frank and liberal in our promises to God, to men, and to ourselves. The poor man says, "Oh, if I had riches, how rich would I be in good works!" The illiterate says, "Oh, that I were learned; what service I would do!" But let us pray that we may have grace to be useful and serviceable with what we have, so that, whether in a narrow or more dilated capacity, we may adorn the doctrine of our God and Savior in all things.

"In all things" means in positive duties as well as negative ones. It is not enough that we do not curse God, we must bless Him. The Pharisees in Luke 18:11 had a religion made of mostly negatives, with a small sprinkling of lesser duties, and not without a mixture of superstition. "God, I thank Thee, I am not as other men are; extortioners, unjust, adulterers, and even as this publican."

When the final sentence shall pass upon every wicked man, it will proceed as in Matthew 25:42: "I was hungry and ye gave Me no meat. I was naked and ye clothed Me not. I was sick and in prison, and ye visited Me not." The indictment will not be laid that they plucked the bread out of the disciples' mouths, but that they did not feed them. Nor will the charge run that they stripped the clothes off the saints' backs, but that they did not clothe them. They are not accused that they cast them into prison, but that they did not relieve them, did not visit them when there. We have all cause to pray with the holy person, "Lord pardon my sins of omission." Negatives will never entitle us to that blessing of living many days and seeing much good. We must join the affirmative with them. Psalm 34:14: "Depart from evil, and do good."

"In all things" means in all companies, whether holy or unholy. The apostle discharges the Corinthians (1 Corinthians 5:9–10) from the company of fornicators. And yet he seems to correct or limit the prohibition: "yet not altogether with the fornicators of this world, or with the covetous, or extortioners, or with idolaters"; for in that latitude the command would not be practical. For then, says he, "ye must needs go out of the world." Either a Christian must retire wholly from all business in the world, or must quite remove his station into the other world. A godly man then may possibly be cast among them, though a prudent man will not of choice frequent them. The holy art and skill is how he may adorn the gospel when he is inevitably thrown among them. And it is a good rule that if we cannot make wicked men ashamed of their wickedness, yet should we neither be ashamed of (nor a shame to) holiness; if they will not go to heaven with us, let us not in complaisance go to hell with them. Though prudence will advise us to be wise as serpents, a good conscience will oblige us to keep ourselves innocent as doves so that our unseasonable rashness may not expose us to the fury of men, nor our temporizing compliance to the wrath of God. David had studied this case with great accuracy. Psalm 39:1–3: "I will keep my mouth with a bridle while the wicked is before me. I was dumb with silence; I held my peace, even from good, and my sorrow was stirred. My heart waxed hot within me; while I was musing the fire kindled, then spake I with my tongue."

There was a notable conflict in David's soul between his prudence and his zeal while the wicked were before him. Prudence advised silence; zeal counseled speech. While the case was desperate, and no hope of doing good appeared, prudence prevailed and he was silent; but as soon as there appeared a fair probability of doing more good than harm, or rather some good and no harm, then zeal unlocked his lips and he spoke with his tongue. A modest word in season, even among the profane, has proved to be a seed of God lodged in the mind which divine grace, in due time, has awakened to conversion.

Let us therefore earnestly beg God for this mixture of holy zeal and holy prudence so that, when providence shall cast our lot into evil company, though we must have some commerce with wicked men's persons, we may have no communion with them in their wickedness. I conclude this heading with that blessed advice of 1 Peter 2:12: "Having your conversation honest among the Gentiles, that whereas they speak against you as evildoers, they may by your good works, which they shall behold, glorify God in the day of visitation." 1 Peter 3:16: "Having a good conscience, that whereas they speak evil of you, as evildoers, they may be ashamed that falsely accuse your good conversation in Christ."

"In all things" means in all those relations wherein the goodness and wisdom of God has placed us. It has pleased the sovereign Disposer of all things, in His own world, which He powerfully made and wisely administers, to set His rational creatures in several relationships. Some He has appointed to govern, others to obey. But whatever post the divine pleasure has allotted us to keep, our business must be to adorn the doctrine of our God and Savior in all things. Romans 12:6–8: "Having therefore gifts differing according to the grace that is given us—whether ministry, let us wait on our one ministering; or he that teacheth on teaching; or he that exhorteth on exhortation; or he that ruleth with diligence," so that we may fill up that relation with a holy zeal to glorify our God and Savior.

There is the master and his servant; the master perhaps may think he is above the control of his poor servant, but he must know that he has also a Master in heaven (Colossians 4:1). Let him then remember that with this God there is no respect of persons. Let them make conscience to give unto their servants that which is just and equal. It is just that they receive the reward of their labor which by compact or desert they may claim. It is equal that, as masters exact of their servants time for their service, they allow them competent time for the service of God; nor let servants think that their relationship to God exempts them from fidelity to their masters on earth, 1 Timothy 6:1: "Let as many servants as are under the yoke count their own masters worthy of all honor, that the name of God and His doctrine be not blasphemed." To plead or pretend Christian liberty as an exemption from Christian subjection and duty, is an open blaspheming of the doctrine of God. But because the case of the servants seems hard, the divine goodness has made the promise adequate to the precept. Colossians 3:23–24: "Whatever ye do, do it heartily as to the Lord; knowing that of the Lord ye shall receive the reward of the inheritance." This exhortation is inculcated in our text and context. Verse 9 exhorts servants to be obedient unto their own masters, and to please them well in all things; not "purloining," but showing all good fidelity, and all upon this great consideration, which has its influence upon all other relations and their respective duties, that they may "adorn the doctrine of God our Savior in all things."

It is upon the same reason and account that wives are strictly commanded in Titus 2:4–5 to be "sober, to love their husbands, to love their children, to be discreet, keepers at home, good, and obedient to their own husbands," and all this enforced with the same great motive, that the Word of God be not blasphemed. All inferior relations carry some inconveniences with them; they have the laboring oar which renders their case somewhat difficult, and furnishes corrupt hearts with matter of discontent. But still this one thing may abundantly satisfy them, that in whatsoever station the wise God has fixed them, they are yet capable of adorning the doctrine of our God and Savior.

This consideration is also pressed upon the consciences of subjects in 1 Peter 2:13–15: "Submit yourselves to every ordinance of man for the Lord's sake, whether it be to the king as supreme, or unto governors, as unto them that are sent by Him; for so is the will of God, that by well-doing ye put to silence the ignorance of foolish men." An abundance of reproach has been thrown in the face of religion on this score, which we can never wash off without tears; it is well it was not washed off with our blood, nor shall we be able to do it, till obedience for conscience's sake shall convince the world that though the ordinance is of man, yet the authority is of God, by which they reign, and for which we obey. Verse 6: "As free, and yet not using our liberty as a cloak of maliciousness, but as the servants of God."

Last, "in all things" means in all those various conditions to which we are prone in this life: plenty or want, sickness or health, a good or evil report, liberty or restraint; in all these, or whatever other diversities of providence the wise God shall try and exercise us with, the gospel of Christ must be regarded and advanced.

As poverty gives no dispensation to murmur, repine, or steal, so riches give no indulgence to oppression, luxury, or riot. The doctrine of the gospel reaches the highest and binds the lowest. Has God favored you with prosperity? Bless His name, but do not humor yourself in vanity. Has God humbled you? Humble yourself under His mighty and righteous hand, that He may exalt you in His due time (1 Peter 5:6).

A garment may be made decent and comely for a funeral as well as a wedding. In prosperity God invites us to rejoice (Ecclesiastes 7:14), but yet to wear our garments of praise with humility. In the day of adversity, we are called to consider that God has set the one over against the other. Of this excellent spirit was the Apostle Paul. Philippians 4:12: "I know both how to be abased and how to abound; everywhere, and in all things, I am instructed both to be full and to be hungry, both to abound and to suffer need." This one instance fairly copied out upon our hearts, and expressed in our walking, would convince the world of the excellency of the doctrine of the gospel and the grace of God, that can teach the soul to maintain an equipoise of mind in all estates; to have a humble heart in an elevated condition, and a high faith in a low one.

Afflictive sorrows and exalting comforts divide our whole lives between them, yet both of them are capable of glorifying God. James 5:13: "If any man be afflicted, let him pray." Prayer under affliction witnesses that we believe our God to be good and gracious in it; that He can support us under it, can do us much good by it, and deliver us from it. "But if any be cheerful, let him sing psalms." Since God has divided our lives between afflictions and consolations, let us divide them between prayer and praise. I conclude with 1 Corinthians 7:29–31: "Brethren, the time is short; it remaineth that they that weep be as though they wept not, and they that rejoice as though they rejoiced not, and they that buy as though they possessed not; for the fashion of this world passeth away." When grace shall teach us a holy indifference of spirit towards these outward things: to mourn under evil circumstances with that moderation, believing that God can turn our sorrow to good, nay into joy; and to rejoice under smiling dispensations, as they who believe our elations and transports may soon be dashed; and to keep that equability of spirit as they who know the fashion of this world passes away—then shall we adorn the doctrine of God our Savior in all things.

4

The Precepts of the Gospel

What are the particulars of the doctrine of this gospel which we must adorn, and how may we adorn it in those particulars?

The doctrine of the gospel may be reduced to two headings, precepts and promises, and both of these may be comprehended under the general term of the divine testimonies, because they testify what God expects from us and what we may expect from God. The preceptive part informs us what God justly expects from us in a way of duty; the promissory part informs us what we may expect humbly yet assuredly from God, either for present assistance or future reward. Both of these, if narrowly considered, will inform us what it is that will adorn the doctrine of the gospel.

I begin with the precepts. These are the true copy of the divine nature, the great instances of the divine authority, the visible demonstrations of the holiness of the Lawgiver, the express image of the purity of Him who gave them forth, and the great proofs of our integrity. A marvelous beauty and glory is impressed upon them by God, but they have been insolently trampled upon by unhallowed feet, cruelly treated by unclean hands, and now how to recover them to their original glory is the difficulty and design of this discourse.

If we ask the psalmist what value and esteem he put upon them, what glory, what beauty he could behold in them, he readily answers in Psalm 119:128: "I esteem all Thy precepts concerning all things to be right, and I hate every false way." *All* Thy precepts concerning *all* things. There is a luster in every single precept, but a glory in them all. As every star shines with its proper light, but as they stand combined in their asterisms and constellations, so they shine with a marvelous glory. And as every creature which God produced by His creative word was good, yet, when He came to take a prospect of them in their relations to each other, He pronounced them "exceeding good" (Genesis 1:31). Such are the precepts of God; and they are so concerning all things. They reach the heart with all its principles and ends; they govern our words; they regulate our lives; they restrain from sin; they constrain to obedience; they instruct us how to walk holily before God, honestly and righteously towards men, soberly towards ourselves, and to hate every false way.

If you again ask him why or upon what reasons he prizes them at this high rate; he will satisfy you. Verse 72: "The law of Thy mouth is better unto me than thousands of gold and silver." I know there may be good use made of gold and silver. A good conscience will not purchase meat in the market, nor will innocence buy us clothing in the shops. But the law of Thy mouth is better, upon higher, upon nobler accounts. It acquaints me with those ways wherein God is to be found; where I may expect communion with Him. It directs me how to walk well pleasing to my God, whom to please is my highest ambition. It shows me how I may be kept from the paths of the destroyer. Gold and silver will not heal a wounded conscience, nor pluck the thorn out of the flesh, nor instruct the doubting soul how to clear up its peace with God. What use others may make of their gold and silver I do not know; but unto me, the words of Thy mouth are better. By them is Thy servant warned to avoid the sin and to escape the snare; by them is Thy servant reproved, when his own folly has exposed him to the bait and snare; and by them is Thy servant recovered out of those temptations into which my own rashness or carelessness have thrown me.

The goodness of all things is reckoned from their suitableness to the present and pressing exigency. If we are hungry, a piece of bread is better than thousands of gold and silver pieces, which we may have and yet starve. If naked, a few rags are better in that present strait than thousands of gold and silver coins, which will not cover our nakedness. If then the mind is uneasy and conscience dissatisfied; if sorrow sits as a thick cloud upon the brow, the Word of God which speaks to the case is better than thousands of gold and silver coins.

There are three things which render the precepts of Christ easy, and our obedience pleasant:

1. When we keep our hearts fixed upon the Author of them. It is the doctrine of God our Savior. As God He claims authority over us; as a Savior He challenges an interest in us. Right to command and interest to obey make a cord of love too strong to be broken. Christ assures us in Matthew 11:29–30 that His yoke is easy and His burden light. It is a yoke (none of Christ's servants are sons of Belial), but it is an easy yoke. The strength which He gives, that principle of love which is the governing principle of the renewed nature, makes it so. Hence Christ presses obedience upon that principle in John 14:15: "If ye love Me, keep My commandments."

Can you pretend a mighty love to any person and yet despise their authority? Give this essential proof of your love, that you keep His commandments. If your friend should soothe you up, and with many fair and fawning compliments protest that he values you, and yet at the same time spit in your face or throw dung upon you, you would desire him to give better evidence of his love than those actions which speak spite and scorn. The commands of Christ are the mounds and fences which He has set about His glory. If you pluck down those walls and defenses which your neighbor has set about his enclosures, and then pretend that you do all this out of pure love and respect for him, I am persuaded that he would desire you to forbear such proofs of your love and give more convincing tokens of it. Christ would rather you spare your high expressions and give evidence of your love by sincere obedience.

2. When the conscience is bound in subjection to Christ, when the soul can lie at His feet and take the law from His mouth, then will His precepts be exceedingly precious. A command that lies only on the back is heavy and ungrateful, and the uneasy soul waits but a fair opportunity to shake it off; and the flesh will never let it lack such an opportunity. But when it has gotten hold upon, and a firm footing in the heart, it meets with a principle there suited to it. The new heart makes new obedience pleasant. Ezekiel 36:26–27: "A new heart also will I give you, and I will put My Spirit within you, and cause you to walk in My statutes; and ye shall keep My judgments, and do them."

3. A clear experience of present strength to obey, with a firm belief of a future reward, will render obedience pleasant. There is not only present strength felt,

and a future reward expected, but a prelibation of that future reward too, which contributes to this delight. Psalm 19:11: "In keeping of them there is great reward." But when the holy soul can live, walk, and act in the hope of that eternal salvation whereof Christ is the Author to all who obey Him (Hebrews 5:9); when the eye of faith has Moses's perspective, to behold Him who is invisible, and clearly see the recompense of reward—this alleviates the burdens, counterbalances the inconveniences, and overcomes the difficulties which attend a close walking with God. A future reward produces a present comfort; the reward of eternity influences the present time for faith and hope, though they deal with what is absent, distant, future, yet administer present joy, present strength, because the connection between upright universal obedience and the glory of that other world is close, strong, and inviolable.

Such are then the precepts of the gospel, so excellent, so glorious in themselves, and to all who in a conscientious course of holy walking have proved and approved them. And yet so shamefully have they been sullied, violated, and trodden under foot that the question recoils upon us at every turn. How shall we vindicate them? What must we do to restore them to their own inherent glory? In answer to which I will lay down these few and plain but necessary directions.

DIRECTION 1. Let the universality of your obedience convince the world that you make conscience of obeying; you will never satisfy others, nor yourselves, nor the Searcher of hearts, to obey in any unless you obey in all. He who will pick out one duty, where and when it may consist with the interest of the flesh, and terest, will never stop the mouths of men, nor silence the clamors of his own conscience, when it shall accuse him of partiality in God's law (Malachi 2:9).

The Lawgiver has stamped the same impressions of His authority, the same characters of holiness, upon them all. And he who can allow himself professedly and deliberately to break one is prepared to break them all when the temptation shall press hard upon his corrupt heart. James 2:11: "He that said, 'Do not commit adultery,' said also, 'Do not kill.' " This was the ground of the psalmist's lifting up his face with confidence in Psalm 119:6: "Then shall I not be ashamed, when I have respect to all Thy commandments."

The scribes and pharisees were sad instances of this hypocrisy. They would strain at a gnat and yet would swallow a camel. They would be thought severe in tithing mint, anise, and cummin, and yet would neglect mercy and judgment, those great and weighty matters of the law (Matthew 23:23). If we look upon them in ceremonials, they were the most straightlaced and tender-conscienced men in the whole world. But when you view them in their morals, they were the most loose and dissolute men (John 18:28). They would not go into the judgment hall lest they should be defiled, but they would go there that they might keep the Passover. And yet they were not so nice, and squeamish, but they could shed innocent blood, and imbrue their hands in that of the Messiah. They would not touch a dead body for all the world, yet did not scruple to murder the man Jesus. They would not eat with unwashed hands, but had no regard to cleanse their consciences. The apostle expostulates with the Judaizers in Romans 2:22–24: "Thou that abhorest idols, dost thou commit sacrilege? Thou that makest thy boast of the law, through breaking of the law, dishonorest thou God? For the name of God is blasphemed among the Gentiles through you."

In a word, nothing will buoy up the repute of a drowning religion till the professors of it shall make it appear that they not only obey the precepts of the gospel, but that they carry a radicated principle in their hearts that will not allow them to disobey; which principle, though it falls short of what God in strictness may expect, yet must come up to what He in mercy will accept. This was the ground of the apostle's confidence in Hebrews 13:18: "Pray for us! For we trust we have a good conscience, in all things, willing to live honestly."

DIRECTION 2. Make it appear that you can and dare obey against all temptations, oppositions, and discouragements. An unsound man will walk smoothly on in smooth ways, but rugged paths and a stiff gale in his face make him return. Thus many will walk a mile or two with Christ, but, when persecution arises because of the Word, they have always a reserve in their bosoms, and an evil heart is an easy casuist to dispense with obedience upon slender penance.

That man who is under a law in his own conscience, subject to the authority of God, who owns no dispensation from obedience nor indulgence to sin is the man who will adorn the precepts.

They who can shift their sails as the wind veers, and use all the points of the compass to make their point, and whether the gale blows from hell or heaven can serve themselves of it, will never credit his religion.

DIRECTION 3. Let us be much in the exercise of

those graces, the practice of those duties, which men understand. Sincere intentions, good meanings, uprightness of heart, or the acting of your faith upon God do not come within their cognizance till you can show and demonstrate your faith by your works. Let your faith justify your persons before God; but until your works shall justify your faith before men, you will never be able to justify your religion and your sincerity therein. Never tell men of your faith in our Lord Jesus Christ. Unless you show repentance from dead works, they will not believe. And this was St. Paul's practice of piety. Acts 24:16: "Herein do I exercise myself, always to keep a conscience void of offense towards God, and towards men." But because this is that convincing point which must, if ever, recover the credit of religion, let me be allowed to prescribe some more general rules for the right and comely ordering of our conversation.

• Be very zealous in God's cause, and meek and yielding in your own. Be content to lie at the footstool, that the honor of God may have the throne. I recommend to you the great example of our blessed Savior: He was a lamb in his own cause and a lion in His Father's. He who could be scourged and not open his mouth could open it in holy indignation and scourge the buyers and sellers out of the temple. He submitted to be called "Beelzebub" (impostor), and whatever opprobrious terms a rancorous heart could vomit upon Him. But in the cause of His God and Father, He could thunder and flash fire in the face of the most obdurate conscience. "Be ye therefore followers of Christ; who when He was reviled, reviled not again; when He suffered threatened not, but committed Himself [and His cause] to Him that judgeth righteously" (1 Peter 2:23).

And again, "Not rendering evil for evil, or railing for railing, but contrariwise blessing, knowing that ye are thereunto called that ye should inherit a blessing" (1 Peter 3:9).

• Be strict and severe to yourselves, but very charitable towards others. Concerning our brethren, we have this rule in Romans 14:13: "Let us not judge one another any more," but concerning ourselves we have 1 Corinthians 11:31: "If we would judge ourselves, we should not be judged." We are incompetent judges of others because we do not know upon what principles our brother may proceed; we cannot take a just measure of the latitude of his understanding by which he governs himself. There we ought to be sparing in our censure, but you may know what is in your own heart, and know more about yourself than all the world knows about thee, or you know about all the world.

It has brought no small scandal upon religion that the professors of it have been sharp-sighted abroad, but blind at home; they could see a mote in their brother's eye, and not the beam in their own, not duly considering that we who exact a few pence from our brother need the forgiveness of many talents from our God (Matthew 18:24).

• Let us abridge ourselves in the use of things which are in their own nature indifferent. He who will go to the utmost length of his rope will easily break it. It is difficult to know where that which is lawful ends and that which is sinful begins. He who will always go as far as he may go shall sometimes go further than he ought to go. How much safer is it to keep a foot within our limits than to go an inch beyond them? Better do less than is lawful than what is sinful. It's an excellent caution the apostle prescribes in Romans 14:16: "Let not your good be evil spoken of." The glory of Christ and the honor of our holy religion teach us to retrench in what is merely lawful; and still let us attend that rule found in Romans 14:21: "It is good neither to eat flesh, nor drink wine, nor anything whereby thy brother stumbleth, or is offended, or is made weak." Three things are included in this canon: (1) that we do not lay a stumbling block before our brother to draw him into sin; (2) that we do not provoke his passion to speak evil of the good ways of God; and (3) that we do not weaken our brother, nor make him weak in his walking with God, by an unseasonable use of our Christian liberty.

• Let your visible righteousness towards men be an inseparable companion of your invisible righteousness before God. With what arguments will you persuade men that you are sincere and upright in His sight if you cannot convince them that you are so in your dealings with them? Romans 12:17: "Provide things honest in the sight of all men." I look upon that man as lost who has lost all regard to the judgment of others, and doubly lost who has cast off all respect to the judgment of his final Judge.

• Be ambitious to have a public spirit. Express the image of Him who is good and does good. The sun does not restrict its beams to its own orb, but shines upon the good and bad. The air does not enclose itself, but lends breath in common to all. The rain is not imprisoned in the clouds, but sheds fruitfulness on the field of the saint and sinner. The ocean supplies the upper and the lower world with its waters. Let us then pray to be made partakers of the promise given to

Abraham in Genesis 12:2: "I will bless thee, and make thee a blessing."

Those little, narrow souls who make themselves their own center and circumference, who dwell within their own shell, and bless themselves that all is well at home, and never look abroad to see how it fares with the oppressed, the fatherless, the widow, the sick, the hungry, and the naked, who do not consider the afflictions of Joseph, are great scandals to a holy religion. They do not imitate the blessed Jesus who, according to Acts 10:38, "went about doing good, and healing all that were oppressed of the devil, for God was with him." Such was the counsel of the apostle in Titus 3:8: "This is a faithful saying, and those things I will that thou affirm constantly, that they which have believed in God be careful to maintain good works; these things are good and profitable unto man." Verse 14: "And let ours also learn to maintain good works for necessary uses, that they be not unfruitful."

• Let the holiness of the inner man shine with a convincing light into all the actions of the outward man. True holiness will diffuse itself into and through the external carriage and demeanor, so that a man shall be forced to say, "God is truly in that soul." As the pride and wantonness of filthy ones steams and reeks through the skin into their apparel, their language, and their converse, so should, so will the humility, meekness, modesty, chastity, and heavenliness of holy ones display itself in their external behavior, especially in food and raiment. 1 Timothy 2:9–10: "That women adorn themselves with modest apparel [the modesty and chastity of the heart will evidence itself in the modesty and chastity of clothing], with shamefacedness and sobriety, not with broidered hair, or gold, or pearls, or costly array; but (which becometh women professing godliness) with good works." For thus, said Peter in 1 Peter 3:5, "did the holy women of old time who trusted in God adorn themselves."

When the favorable providence of God shall exalt you, do not forget whence you have been raised. Do not forget those you have left behind you; do not forget yourself or your God. It has brought much reproach upon religion that many professors change their tempers with their outward circumstances; and when they have gotten more sail, they throw away their ballast. Such was Jeshurun in Deuteronomy 32:15: "Who when he waxed fat, forsook the Lord, lightly esteemed and was unmindful of the Rock of his salvation."

• Maintain a high and noble faith in a low estate. It is convincing to men that there is something real and solid in the doctrine of the gospel when, though the fig tree does not blossom, though there is no fruit in the vine, though the labors of the olive fail and the fields yield no increase, yet can rejoice in the Lord and triumph in the God of their salvation (Habakkuk 3:17–18).

5

The Promises of the Gospel

The promises testify of what we may expect from God, and upon this head I will open two things. I will briefly open the nature of the promises, and then show what conversation will adorn the doctrine of the gospel, as it is contained in the promises.

A promise may be described as a testimony which God has given of Himself through Christ, to secure our faith in whatever we may expect from Him. As a precept testifies what God expects from us, so a promise testifies what we may expect from Him. The glory of the New Covenant is that what we expect from God enables us to perform what He expects from us. It is in the strength of the promise that we are enabled to obey the precept. It is another excellency of this covenant that divine mercy has annexed the promise to the precept, and so we are not left to a naked law. The same apostle who complains (2 Corinthians 3:5) of an insufficiency to think anything of himself, can yet boast that he can do all things through Christ who strengthens him (Philippians 4:13). Nothing in himself, but all things in Christ. The command creates our duty, but the promise affords strength for obedience. Again, according to the extent of the promises must be the extent of our expectation. What length God has gone in promising, the same length may we go in praying, believing, and hoping.

As the precepts are the bounds of our duty, and all that we can pretend beyond them is superstitious folly, so the promises are the limits of our faith; and to expect beyond them is presumption. Further, we cannot justly complain that we are narrowed and restrained in the wideness of the promises, for they are adequate to the spiritual necessities of all His children in all ages. The oil in the cruise will run while there is a vessel to receive it; our God has to give while we can find a heart to pray and receive. Mercy and grace will never fail while there is room to receive it. It was on this consideration that the psalmist, weighing the indigence of his soul and the exigency of his condition, was well willing to accept the promises for his supply and treasure. Psalm 119:111: "Thy testimonies have I taken for a heritage forever, for they are the rejoicing of my heart"—so many promises, so many testimonies what God will do for His children, what He will bestow on them, and what they may expect from Him.

Now David, we see, could securely take God's single security, nor required any to be bound with him for performance. What security God gave, that he took with the hand, with the arms of faith, as those ancient worthies did who are spoken of in Hebrews 11:13, who died in the faith, not having received the promises, but having seen them afar off, and were persuaded of them, and embraced them. There are two things in the promises: the goodness contained in them and the truth that confirms them. Those eminent saints received the truth, though God kept the goodness still in His own hands. And thus the psalmist accepted God's testimonies for good payment though the grace, mercy, and glory wrapped up in them were chiefly of things future, distant, and invisible. These he took for a heritage; he blessed himself and rejoiced that the lines were fallen unto him in pleasant places, and that he had a goodly heritage (Psalm 16:6). Give him but a clear interest in them, and he is content that the men of the world, whose portion lies there, should divide the world among themselves. For they are the rejoicing of his heart. They are light in darkness, comfort in trouble, advice in straits, ease in pain, supply in want, health in sickness, and life in death.

But that I may more fully and distinctly give you the theory of these exceeding great and precious promises, there are two things in them which shall be more particularly considered: the fullness of the promises and the faithfulness of the promises.

First, the fullness of the promises. They contain whatsoever the soul upon spiritual accounts can possibly need. They are commensurate to the necessities of the saints in all cases. The promise made to Abraham in Genesis 17:7 ("I will establish My covenant between Me and thee, to be a God to thee") has been frequently exemplified in later times. 2 Corinthians 6:16: "I will be their God." And it includes all that God can promise, all that the soul can ask or receive. As it is great folly to sit down with any promise of God that is short of Himself, so it is as great a folly to aspire after anything beyond Him. As a little piece of gold may be beaten out to a great breadth, or drawn out to an incredible length, yet it is still the same gold for weight and substance, though it will be more for use. So may this comprehensive promise be drawn out into infinite particulars, but still all of them are but this one: "I will be thy God." The Almighty God will be your strength, the all-wise God your conduct, and the everliving God your life.

But if we desire more explicit satisfaction, God has given it in 1 Timothy 4:8: "Godliness hath the promise of the life that now is, and that which is to come." Will this world, will the other world, will both worlds satisfy you? Will time and eternity content you? This word testifies what you may expect from the promise.

Second, the faithfulness of God in the promises. I recommend these things to your observation:

God's faithfulness in the promise is God Himself, clothing Himself with the attribute that our faith may more easily take hold on Him and more securely rely on Him. God is full and faithful. He is fullness and faithfulness. God seems to value Himself especially upon this attribute. Psalm 138:2: "Thou hast magnified Thy Word above all Thy name." Whatever else may fail, He will not allow His faithfulness to fail. Psalm 89:34–35: "His covenant He will not break, nor alter the thing that is gone out of His lips; for He hath sworn by His holiness that He will not lie unto David." Hence it is that I say unbelief is a sin of such horrid guilt, because it dishonors God in that point of which He is so jealous and tender. God can no more lie than He can die; to doubt or deny His faithfulness is to doubt or deny His being. 1 John 5:10: "He that believeth not God has made Him a liar." Every thought, word, or act that represents God otherwise than He is casts a reproach upon the divine majesty; but to make Him a liar, which unbelief does, represents Him as if He were that evil one (John 8:44), who is a liar, and the father of lies. It is true, none can make God a liar any more than they can make light darkness, or truth falsehood; but the unbe-

liever who does not credit the testimony of God, by in-
terpretation and devilish construction, either judges
Him so to be, or represents Him as such to others. And
this truth, this faithfulness of God, is the great buttress
of the promise. "In hope of eternal life, which God, that
cannot lie, hath promised before the world began"
(Titus 1:2).

This faithfulness of God in the promise is now
drawn up into writing. God has not only spoken but
written. We have it not only from His mouth, but under
his hand, which, though it adds nothing to divine
truth, yet it contributes much to our weak faith. For
hereby we have a more steady aim at the mind and will
of God than if it had been conveyed only by a voice
from heaven, or otherwise. As the law was more durably
engraven upon the two tables than when delivered
from Mount Sinai, how much more is our security that
God proceeds with us, and we treat with Him, by a written word than if we had been left to the uncertainly of
oral tradition. Our blessed Savior assures us in John
10:35 that the Scriptures cannot be broken. Though
nothing is more easy than to violate a precept, yet nothing is more impossible than to repeal it; unbelief disparages the promise, but cannot make it void. As a river
meets with rocks and mountains that would obstruct its
course and current, and may sometimes run under
ground, yet it will make its way through all opposition.
Psalm 100:5: "Thy truth endureth through all genera-
tions."

The truth of God in the promise receives yet a further confirmation from the oath of God. As when God
had nothing greater to give He gave Himself, His Son,
and His Spirit in an everlasting covenant, so, when he

had nothing greater to confirm that covenant by, He swore by Himself. Hebrews 6:17: "Wherein God, willing more abundantly to show unto the heirs of promise the immutability of His counsel, confirmed it by an oath." Happy is the man for whose sake God will vouchsafe to swear! Miserable is the man who will not believe a swearing God! How wretched in the nature of suspicion, jealousy, and doubt is he whom the highest security direct and collateral, even from veracity and infallibility, cannot satisfy.

The truth of the promises is yet further attested, sealed, and ratified by the death of Christ. Of His blood and cross though there are other and greater ends, yet this is one to confirm the promises. Romans 15:8: "Jesus Christ a minister of circumcision for the truth of God, to confirm the promises made to the fathers." And that the promise might be sure to all the seed (Romans 4:16), He has drawn the covenant into a testamentary form, and then died to seal and ratify his own testament. Hebrews 9:17: "A testament is of force after men are dead, otherwise it is of no strength while the testator liveth."

You have had many gracious experiences afforded of the faithfulness of God in the promises; enter them upon record in your souls: an answer to prayer, the pardon of sin sealed to the conscience, present help in time of need, suitable and seasonable strength against temptations, eminent deliverances in pressing dangers—these are so many earnests of what He will further do, special tokens of His truth in doing them.

In all your dealings with men you will buy a sample or pattern; many of these we have had, and from one we might conclude what He will perform in all other cases. He shows us in little things what He will do in great ones; and by what He performs in one instance gives hope of what He will do in all the rest. 2 Corinthians 1:10: "He hath delivered us, and doth deliver us, in whom we trust that He will yet deliver us." So that we may with the prophet set up our Ebenezer (1 Samuel 7:12), and give it this inscription: "Hitherto hath the Lord helped us."

God summons us in upon our consciences to give testimony to His faithfulness in the promises. Isaiah 43:12: "I have declared and saved, I have showed when there was no strange god among you; therefore ye are My witnesses." God will bring our former experiences to confront our present fears. Therefore be well advised, if it is so heinous a sin to bear false witness against your neighbor, what is it to bear false witness against your God?

6

How We Adorn the Doctrine of the Gospel

God has sealed to the promises with His truth, His word, and His oath. Let us now mutually seal them with our faith. John 3:33: "He that receiveth His testimony hath set to his seal that God is true." It is the highest disparagement to a person of known integrity not to receive his testimony; and yet man, by departing from his God, has forfeited his credibility. David once said in a hot fit of passion, in his haste, that all men were liars (Psalm 116:11), all men, even the prophets who encouraged him in the name of the Lord. The apostle deliberately has asserted in Romans 3:4: "Let God be true, and every man a liar." As none is absolutely good but One, so none is true perfectly but One, and that is God. Now if we can receive the witness of man, who is branded upon record as being a liar, that he goes astray as soon as he is born, speaking lies (Psalm 58:3), what a reproach do we cast upon God, who is the truth, all whose promises are "yea and amen in Christ to the glory of God" (2 Corinthians 1:20). And thus the apostle argues in 1 John 5:9, "If we receive the witness of men [as we must], the witness of God is greater." And if an oath among men for confirmation is to them an end of all strife (Hebrews 6:16), let the promise of God, confirmed by His oath, put an end to all those controversies which our suspicious hearts have made. Let us come off roundly with God, put our seal to His promises, and make all the world know to its shame that we have a God whom we can securely trust.

In pursuance of this, let us walk cheerfully before the world upon the credit and security of the promises. There was a time when holy Job could walk in darkness by the light of God (Job 29:3), when the light of the promises guided and comforted him in the darkness of providences; when though all was gloomy without, yet all was clear within. It is a great blemish that professors give the face of their religion; that we hear much and often of their complaints, but seldom of their praises. They are always mourning, never rejoicing. This represents religion as a melancholy, cloudy thing, and frightens strangers from all acquaintance with it; whereas, if we lived up to the height of what our religion would justify us, we might glory in tribulations (Romans 5:3), rejoice evermore (1 Thessalonians 5:16), and give thanks to God, who always causes us to rejoice and triumph in Christ (2 Corinthians 2:14). Nor would this be any triumphing before the victory, seeing we are already more than conquerors in Him who loved us (Romans 8:37). For what could all our outward afflictions, tribulations, crosses, losses, or the disappointments that we meet with in the world do to extinguish our joy if we, as we might, urge the promises upon our own hearts, plead them with God, and object them to the tempter.

We might urge them upon our own dejected souls. Psalm 43:5: "Why art thou cast down, O my soul, and why art thou disquieted within me? Hope in God, for I shall yet praise Him." We are apt to be cast down and disquieted when we are not able to assign a good reason for the dejection and disquiet. We have a God to trust in, a word from that God by which to lay hold on Him, so why are we then cast down? And this psalmist at other times has been able to relieve himself from such a word. Psalm 119:50: "This is my comfort in my affliction, for Thy word hath quickened me."

We might plead the word of promise with God, and humbly press His own truth upon Himself. Psalm 119:49: "Remember Thy word unto Thy servant, on which Thou hast caused me to hope." It is as if he had said, "Holy Lord! Thou hast encouraged me to hope, and I have Thy word for the ground of that encouragement. I am Thy servant to whom this promise is made, and have therefore reason to apply the word to my own case. And wilt Thou forget Thy word, and fail a servant of Thine who hopes upon Thy security? If Thou had never promised I would never have hoped; but since Thou hast caused me to hope, answer my hope. If I could not say in sincerity, 'Lord, I serve Thee,' I could not say in faith, 'Lord, save me!' If I had forgotten Thy precepts, I could not plead with Thee to remember Thy promises." It was therefore excellent counsel that Chrysostom gave: "Hear thy God in His precepts, that He may hear thy prayers." For although the truth of God is the security of our believing, yet sincere obedience is the ground of our applying to ourselves the promises.

We have the word of promise to answer and repel all the objections of the tempter. His great design is to undermine and blow up that great fundamental principle, that God is good and faithful; that He is good and gracious in all His ways and works, faithful and true in all His words, and great advantage He has gotten this way over many holy ones. David was ready to

conclude in Psalm 77:8 that God's mercy was gone forever, that there was a total and a final failure of the divine goodness, and that His promise failed forever-
more. Now when the wicked one prevails thus, we are
driven from our anchor, floating and hulling upon the
waters, exposed to the next storm, to be dashed in
pieces against the rocks. To all these suggestions and
injections, we have this one answer from 1 Corinthians
10:13: "God is faithful, who will not suffer us to be
tempted above what we are able."

Make all who observe you confess that you dare venture, and if the will of God is so, lay down and lose all
your outward concerns upon the sole insurance and
counter-security of the promises. God does try us sometimes to see how much we dare ensure upon His Word.
Matthew 19:29: "Every one that has forsaken houses, or
brethren, or sisters, or father, or mother, or wife, or
children, or lands, for My name's sake, shall receive a
hundredfold, and shall inherit everlasting life." Here
you easily observe that the promise is large enough,
and the title unquestionably good; the only question is
whether we dare venture our all upon this security. He
who lends money will be satisfied in two points: first,
whether the mortgage offered will bear and answer the
sum he lends upon it; second, whether the title of the
estate is good, what warranty will be given. Now in both
these we have the clearest satisfaction imaginable.
There can be no dispute whether the matter of this
promise will answer whatever we can possibly venture
upon it, for a hundredfold and everlasting life is far
more than we can lay down. Nor can there be any question about the clearness of the title, since Christ Himself undertakes to make it good. If therefore we believe,

how freely, how cheerfully shall we lay down our all at His feet, with them in Hebrews 10:34 who not only patiently but joyfully took the spoiling of their goods, knowing in themselves that they have in heaven a better and enduring substance.

Last, live the life of faith, and despise this poor, beggarly life of sense in comparison to it. The life of sense has its proper food, its comforts, supports, and supplies; it has its employments, its hopes, its trade, and gains. But they are all low and mean, all within the rod and reach of sense. The life of faith has its food too, its joys, its hopes, business, and designs; but these lie out of the road and way of the flesh. Now if we could, through the grace of God, make future invisible things our all, and conform our hearts, our ways, and our course of life to the great end, we would effectually persuade men that the doctrine of the gospel is a most glorious doctrine. Our blessed Savior tells His disciples in John 4:34 that He had meat to eat which they knew not of. As a believer has a hidden life, so he has hidden meat to support it. He has a hidden life. Colossians 3:3: "Your life is hid with Christ in God." And he has hidden food. Revelation 2:17: "To him that overcometh, I will give to eat of the hidden manna." As he has secret sorrows which the world knows nothing of, so has he hidden joys. Proverbs 14:10: "The heart knoweth its own bitterness, and a stranger doth not intermeddle with his joy." And hence it is that the world knows little or nothing of the bread he eats, the life he lives, or the joy he enjoys. 1 John 3:1: "Therefore the world knoweth us not, because it knew Him not." Whatever is within the compass of sense and flesh, the natural man understands; that he values, prizes, relishes, and blesses himself in, because he finds a suitableness between them and his own frame. But if those who profess themselves to be believers have nothing more than this to produce, they hope in vain to persuade others of the excellency of their religion.

Let us therefore give all diligence to get such a view of the glory of that unseen world, as may dash out of countenance all the glittering glory of this, and make it appear by our conversation that we can, with a holy scorn, trample upon present, visible, earthly perishing things, so that, living by faith and not by sense, our hearts may be in heaven where our treasure is, and our conversation in heaven where our hearts are.

7

Reasons to Adorn the Gospel

We come now to the fourth general heading, the only thing remaining before we come to the application. Here let me give the reasons why everyone who professes the gospel of Christ should conscientiously labor to adorn the doctrine of it in all things. The reasons assigned will be very few; let us pray that the good Spirit would make them very strong.

REASON 1. It ought to be our great care to adorn the doctrine of the gospel because it is the doctrine of the great God. It is a doctrine that was given forth from Him that has absolute power to command us. John 7:16: "The doctrine is not Mine, but His that sent Me," and therefore we are to receive it and entertain it as such. 1 Thessalonians 2:13: "Ye received it not as the word of men, but as it is in truth the Word of God." The reproach cast upon the Word of God is cast upon the Author of it, God Himself. Romans 2:23–24: "Through breaking of the law, dishonorest thou God? For the name of God is blasphemed among the Gentiles through you." The affront offered to the laws reflects upon the Lawgiver; and God is concerned in honor to vindicate the dishonor cast upon His own laws. These things are drawn into a narrow compass, and we may enlarge upon them with ease in our own hearts. Let us be well advised whether we are not bound in conscience to vindicate the name of God by adorning this doctrine, which has been so horribly blasphemed by defacing it. He who spits in the face of religion spits in the face of God. He who tramples upon the Word tramples under foot the Son of God.

REASON 2. It is the doctrine of our Savior, our Redeemer; and these terms carry strong obligations in them to adorn His doctrine (or, having already defiled it, to repair the damage we have done to it). The former reason was drawn from authority, but this from interest, and both of them work by love. Christ is a Savior, and has preached the doctrine of salvation. As a Redeemer, He has revealed the doctrine of redemption. As a Mediator, He has made known how sinners may come unto God by Him. It was St. Augustine's censure of the Platonists, "They saw their country, but did not know the way to it." They had at least some rude, confused notions that blessedness must be in the enjoyment of a perfect, infinite being, but they were at a loss how to attain reconciliation and communion with Him. What they saw in a glass darkly, the gospel has revealed plainly, and we see it with open face (2 Corinthians 3:18). What they were totally ignorant of, we behold in a clear sight; that is, wherein our everlasting happiness consists, and how we may reach that happiness. And shall we tread under our feet that blessed doctrine, the power whereof in our hearts will certainly save us, and the guilt lying upon our head will eternally condemn us?

The apostle's pleading is clear and strong in 1 Corinthians 6:19–20: "Ye are not your own, for ye are bought with a price that ye may glorify Him in your spirits and bodies, which are His." It is an acknowledged piece of justice that he who purchases lawfully should enjoy peaceably; and with what indignation do we exclaim against that man who keeps out of possession a lawful purchaser. Consider this case, for it is your own: if Christ has bought you with an invaluable price, whose true value none can perfectly understand but the Father to whom it was paid, shall we treat that gospel which brings us these glad tidings with contempt and neglect?

REASON 3. To adorn the doctrine of our God and Savior will be our own greatest ornament. Holiness was the comely wear of primitive Christianity; no artificial dress did ever so adorn its profession and professors as plain godliness. The varnish and paint of art will wash off with a little stormy weather, but wisdom makes the face to shine (Ecclesiastes 8:1). This is the counsel of divine wisdom (Proverbs 1:8–9): "My son, hear the instruction of thy father, and forsake not the law of thy mother; for it shall be an ornament of grace to thy head, and chains to thy neck." This was the attire wherewith the holy women of old time adorned themselves (1 Peter 3:4), even the ornament of a meek and quiet spirit, which in the sight of God is of great price. Such was the dress of the gospel before the commonness of vain modes and wanton fashions took away the deformity of pride, and almost forced the ancient simplicity to retire into corners.

If we saw an ancient piece of art, drawn by the hand of some of the great masters of Greece or Italy, we would admire the painting, though perhaps ridicule the antique garbs. Surely if some of the primitive professors should rise from the dead, they would neither know us, nor we them. A heavenly conversation is antiquated; everyone wears the livery of his party, the distinguishing Shibboleth of his own sect. But where are they who accommodate themselves in all things to the doctrine according to godliness! What an honor to be a citizen of the New Jerusalem! To be an heir of God, and a joint heir with Christ, his elder brother. Let us endeavor to reflect some of the honor back again upon the gospel which we receive from it.

REASON 4. To adorn the doctrine of the gospel will greatly recommend it to those who are at present strangers to it. We have the prejudices of men to contend with, their radicated enmities to subdue and conquer; we dispute, we argue in vain. It is a severe, uniform holiness, suited to the principles, precepts, and promises, that must either wrest their weapons out of their hands or make them freely lay down their arms at the foot of a Redeemer. In 1 Peter 3:1, the apostle supposes a very hard case: that a believing wife is unequally yoked to an unbelieving husband, which is not an easy condition! But how may it be remedied? The apostle answers, "If any obey not the word, they may be won by the conversation of the wives." But the question is, what conversation will reach that end? He answers again, "While they behold your chaste conversation coupled with fear."

Are there any of you who have a neighbor, a relation, or a friend who is as your own soul; for whose conversion you have longed, prayed, mourned, and added countless entreaties to your prayers and tears? Add a holy humble conscientious conversation, keeping your consciences void of offense toward God and men, and do not despair of success.

REASON 5. Nothing more provokes the wrath of God than to throw dirt in the face of the gospel; and the next provocation is not to wipe that off which others have thrown upon it. Which way God will vindicate His insulted honor, which way He will avenge Himself upon a careless, loose, or indifferent generation of professors, I cannot foretell. He may take the sword into His provoked hand, or give a commission to fire, plague, or other judgment to avenge the quarrel of His gospel. But one thing is certain: He will do it. Leviticus 26:25: "I will bring a sword upon you, that shall avenge the quarrel of My covenants; and when you are gathered together in your cities, I will send the pestilence amongst you; and ye shall be delivered into the hands of your enemies."

We have notoriously affronted the gospel of our God and Savior, either by unmerciful persecution or an unsuitable conversation. This gospel has just cause of quarrel against us. God takes the quarrel of His despised truths, precepts, promises, and ordinances, into His own hands. He will avenge it. He has already sent us a challenge, nay, He has drawn blood on us; yet His patience waits and strives with us, and calls us to take up the controversy. What will we do? Either we must fight it out and carry on a vigorous war against heaven, or entertain it. Oh, that we would entertain better, wiser counsels, and agree with our adversary quickly while we are in the way with him, and he in the way. Let us then repent and turn to the Lord with our whole heart; let us reform our persons, families, our lives, peradventure the Lord may be, nay, certainly the Lord will be reconciled to us, and have mercy upon us.

8

The Application

Only the improvement of the point remains, and till we have done that we have done nothing. But here we usually err. We think it is only the preacher's work to make application when it is the proper duty of all to apply it. All the preacher can do is to direct how it may and must be applied by all who hear it.

This truth must be applied and improved two ways: by way of humiliation and by way of exhortation.

USE OF HUMILIATION. Are we then thoroughly convinced that it ought to be the cautious care of all who profess the gospel to adorn the doctrine of it in all things? Let us then be humbled! Let us take up a bitter lamentation over this bleeding, gasping, and, if grace does not prevent, this dying gospel. It has fared among us just as the poor man in Luke 10:30, who went down from Jerusalem to Jericho, and fell among thieves. They stripped him, wounded him, and left him half dead. But who could expect better quarter from bloody thieves? In this dying and desperate state, there came a priest; he saw him, but his eyes did not affect his heart, so he passed by. A Levite came next; he bestowed a careless look upon him, but passed by on the other side. Might not better things have been expected from the priests and Levites? Well, in the agony and pangs of death, a Samaritan came by, one abhorred by both priest and Levite; one whom they damned as a wretched schismatic. Yet he had bowels of compassion for the expiring man; he bound up his wounds and took care for his cure.

The gospel of God our Savior lies here bleeding and dying! It is in vain to inquire who has been the assassin, who has committed the massacre. For all will remove the guilt from themselves, though all are guilty. In the meantime, religion bleeds on, and is ready to give up the ghost! Now it is usual, when a person is found wounded in the streets, to ask, "Who wounded him?" At least to describe them by such characters so that they may be pursued, seized, and brought to condign punishment. But have we courage enough, conscience enough, to ask wounded religion this question? How readily would it answer, though with the accents of a languishing voice, "It was you, all, and every one of you who are guilty." Our own consciences will accuse and convict us that we are the men!

When our Savior, in Matthew 26:21–22, told His apostles that one of them would betray Him, they were exceedingly sorrowful and began to say one by one, "Lord, is it I? Lord, is it I?" He who knows his own deceitful heart, and the corruption that lies dormant there, will find reason to suspect that a temptation may awaken it to deny his Lord, nay, to betray and fell his Lord and Savior. Peter, James, and John all suspected themselves as much as Judas. And every one of us has cause to say, "Lord, was it I? Was it I who denied Thy truth? Was it I who blemished Thy gospel?" If so, oh, let us mourn bitterly over Him whom we have pierced, as "one that mourneth for an only son" (Zechariah 12:10).

It was a cutting word that would have wounded the heart of anyone but an obdurate Judas: "Judas, betrayest

thou the Son of Man with a kiss?" Do we pretend to kiss
Him, and yet basely betray Him? The smiling face aggravates the rancor of the false heart. It was the base-
ness of Joab that he saluted Abner and then stabbed
him. Do we compliment Christ, and then stab Him?

The gospel may say to us in what was said in the
language of that prophetic scheme in Zechariah 13:6.
The question was asked, "What are those wounds in
thine hands?" Religion will answer, "Those with which
I was wounded in the house of my friends." This
wounds deeper than the swords, the nails, the spear,
and the thorns that wounded Christ. He has been
wounded in the house of His friends! Let not our deceitful hearts think to evade the charge by saying,
"Lord, when did I buffet Thee or spit on Thee? It was
the soldiers! When did I crown Thee with thorns, put a
reed into Thy hands, nail Thee to the cross, or pierce
Thy side with a spear? It was the Jews who accused Thee,
Pilate who condemned Thee, and the soldier who
pierced Thee."

To this Christ will say, "Nay, it was you! You pretended to submit to My scepter, but made it but a broken reed. It was you who professed much love with your
lips, and yet were false to My honor and interest. You
betrayed Me! You called Me 'Lord and Master,' and yet
disobeyed My commandments." And if Christ and His
gospel find no fairer quarter from friends, what may He
expect when He falls into the hands of thieves?

It cut David to the heart to be so treacherously dealt
with by a pretending friend. Psalm 41:9: "Mine own familiar friend in whom I trusted, that did eat of my
bread, hath lifted up his heel against me." May not we
take up the same heavy and doleful complaint on be-

half of religion? They who have eaten her bread and drank her wine have kicked and spurned at her. Hear the psalmist again, mournfully bewailing his case, in Psalm 55:12–14: "It was not an enemy that reproached me, for then I could have borne it; neither was it he that hated me that did magnify himself against me, then I would have hid myself from him. But it was thou, a man, mine equal, my guide, my acquaintance. We took sweet counsel together, and walked to the house of God in company." This was the cutting, killing stroke! And this aggravates the case of religion in this dismal day. Religion has been wounded, betrayed, and reproached by pretended friends, when yet the upright, like that holy, dying woman in 1 Samuel 4:22, do not know how to outlive the departing glory, but are willing to die with it. It is a matter of the greatest difficulty to persuade us to repent of our guiltiness in this thing, and before I can hope to prevail, I must premise a few particulars:

Whatever reproach the professors of religion draw upon their own persons will certainly be fastened upon their profession. Now though this is an unjust procedure, to reproach a holy truth because he who owns it holds it in unrighteousness, yet thus it will be; the crimes and excesses of men reflect upon the doctrine. They who will reproach men for their duties will much more revile them for their iniquities, and from thence take a welcome occasion to revile their principles and professions.

Whatever reproach falls upon religion will reflect upon the Author of it, even our blessed Savior Himself. This should sway all our consciences to walk inoffensively, to give no just occasion to them who seek and watch to blaspheme the name of our God. Hear how affectionately the psalmist prays in Psalm 69:6: "Let not them that wait on Thee, O Lord, be ashamed for my sake; let not them that wait on Thee be confounded for my sake, O Lord God of Israel." And he had reason to be sensible that some precious souls might be justly offended at him and reproached for him, when by his sin he had caused the enemies of God to blaspheme (2 Samuel 12:14).

But that I may more effectually prosecute this use in inviting you to humiliation for and lamentation over those scandals which our holy religion has contracted upon our account, I will endeavor to lay before you these three things: (1) I will show what an excellent religion we have reproached; (2) I will lay before you the great zeal of the primitive Christians to adorn their religion in those purest times; and (3) I will further open how unworthily we have defiled it in ours.

1. Let me show you what an excellent religion we have thus shamefully reproached. Among the many great and glorious excellencies of the Christian religion as it stands described and recorded in the Scriptures of truth, this is one: It is a sound doctrine. 1 Timothy 6:3 speaks of wholesome words, such as are sound in themselves, and made sound. Titus 2:1: "Speak thou the things which become sound doctrine." It is all sound, all sincere, nothing rotten.

This doctrine imbibed will make a sound head, not filling it with empty notions or airy speculations, much less with rotten matter which will breed impostumes and break out into ulcers, but with such due conceptions of God as will settle our faith, engage our fear, provoke our love, command our obedience and secure the soul's everlasting interest.

It will make a sound heart. The psalmist prays in Psalm 119:80, "Let my heart be sound in Thy statutes, that I may not be ashamed." As the truth received into the head will keep us sound from heterodoxy, so the same truth entertained in its power into the heart will secure it from hypocrisy.

It will make a sound conscience; for herein alone is that doctrine of peace and reconciliation with God revealed through Christ, whose blood sprinkled on the conscience purges it from dead works to serve the living God (Hebrews 9:14).

It will produce sound conduct. It is a rule that religion which begins in hypocrisy will end in apostasy. And there's little difference whether we go in a true way with a false heart or forsake that way through a false heart; a sound heart is the great preservative against both.

Now here we have cause to mourn till we have exhausted the springs of tears and can weep no more, lamenting over the rotten doctrines of our days which have defied and defaced this holy and sound doctrine, the rotten conversations that have shamed it and rendered it contemptible. The truth is, we can neither bear our remedy nor our disease; we are sick with our food and sick with our medicine. The Scripture gives us true notions of God, but men are ignorant and too proud to be taught. 1 Timothy 6:4 speaks of being proud, but knowing nothing. This doctrine would be a lamp to our feet, but we shut out eyes against it; it would be a light to our paths, but we will not use it, nor admit it to be our guide in the ways of holiness.

Another excellency of the gospel is that it is a doc-

trine according to godliness (1 Timothy 6:3), and a
doctrine after godliness (Titus 1:1). It is as if the whole
system of divine truth were squared and modeled by
godliness. It is not only true that godliness must be
tried and proved by this doctrine, but that the doctrine
is formed and fashioned by the rule of godliness. Every
leaf, line, and proposition is adapted to the advancement of godliness. There is no indulgence here for sin,
no toleration for lust, not one loose principle in the
body of Scripture divinity. And if any doctrine offers itself that does not breathe purity, we may safely reject it
as that which is not after godliness.

Let this also renew our lamentation that such a doctrine has been tortured upon the rack of unsanctified
wits to abet filthiness and uncleanness. Men have
reaped what God never sowed, and gathered what the
Holy Spirit never strewed, when this grace of the gospel
is turned into lasciviousness and men have abounded
in sin because the grace of God has abounded towards
sinners.

The gospel has this peculiar excellency, that in every respect it is good and profitable to men. It is calculated expressly according to the image of Him who is
good and does good (Psalm 119:68). Such is this holy
doctrine; it is a sanctifying and a saving doctrine.
Proverbs 4:1–2: "Hear, ye children, attend to know understanding, for I give you good doctrine; forsake ye
not my law." This doctrine reveals eternal life, and the
only way to it; it discovers what we must know so that we
do not perish in ignorance; what we must believe so
that we do not perish in infidelity; what we must do so
that we do not perish by disobedience, and what we
must avoid so that we do not perish in our rashness. It

reveals the end of creation, redemption, and how to reach the end of our faith, hope, and prayers in the enjoyment of God, blessed forever to eternity. But if you would have the particulars in which it is good and profitable laid before you at once, read 2 Timothy 3:16–17: "All Scripture is given by inspiration of God, and is profitable for doctrine, for reproof, for correction, for instruction in righteousness, that the man of God may be perfect, thoroughly furnished unto all good works."

And upon this account, if our eyes were rivers, and our heads a fountain of tears, we could not mourn enough that men have turned God's glory into shame (Psalm 4:2). The divine glory has displayed itself gloriously in the gospel: the glory of His mercy manifested to lost (self-lost) sinners; the glory of His justice manifested and satisfied in His Son; the glory of His holiness shining out in the precepts; the glory of His truth shining out in the promises, the glory of His wisdom manifested in adjusting all interests and answering all the pretensions of the holy law—and yet all these are impiously turned into shame.

2. I wish to show the zeal of the primitive Christians to adorn their religion. In those purest times, religion had another face than it now wears. It was delivered pure to them by Christ and His apostles. They represented it suitably to the worst of their enemies, and these things were their glory:

First, there was nothing more eminently found among them than love without dissimulation. The heathen among whom they dwelt could not but say, "Oh, how these Christians love one another" (Acts 2:1). They were all together with one accord in one house, as if one soul animated so many bodies. They were of one heart, one lip, and one shoulder, that they might bear one another's burdens, and so fulfill the law of Christ (Galatians 6:2).

A second excellency in them was their fervent zeal for the honor of their Redeemer; a zeal so hot that it quenched the flames and the heat of the fires which devoured their bodies. This they copied from Christ, the grand examplar of holy zeal for His Father's glory. John 2:17: "The zeal of Thy house hath eaten Me up." Christ's time for sleep, food, and rest was all eaten up by His holy zeal to do His Father's will and finish His work. Such was the original which they propounded to themselves for imitation, and they wrote after it with great exactness; they minded and pursued more the concerns of their Lord than their own. The public interest of the church drowned their own private little interests. As the sun, shining upon our culinary fires, extinguishes them, so did their zeal for Christ burn up all those petty animosities which, when peace and rest from persecution indulged them, broke out into dividing and consuming flames.

Third, it was their glory that they lived in a continual waiting for and expectation of the coming of their Lord. That glorious day, though they could not hasten it, yet their longing, praying souls hastened unto it. 2 Peter 3:12: "Looking for, and hastening unto the coming of the day of God." How they patiently waited, and yet passionately prayed, "Come, Lord Jesus, come quickly" (Revelation 22:20). They longed to see their Lord upon His throne, to see all the kingdoms of the world brought into subjection to the King of saints; and their preparations were answerable to their expectations, making ready for the blessed appearance of their blessed Savior.

Fourth, their discourses and their lives savored of heaven; their conversation was above, whence they looked for their Savior. When their persecutors stripped them of all the accommodations of their pilgrimage, they would say with scorn, "We do but ease you of what you say is your burden and impediment in running your race." And others, when they dragged them to the stake and fire would scoff, "We do but send you where you long and pray to go."

How wretchedly we have copied out those excellencies. All the world sees better than they who have most cause to be ashamed. If we had holy Paul's heart we would shed his tears. Philippians 3:18: "Many walk (of whom I have told you often, and now tell you weeping) that they are enemies of the cross of Christ, who mind earthly things." An earthly conversation bears the clearest contradiction to a heavenly revelation. And now what would dry up the apostle's tears, or what would wipe off this filth from the face of religion, but that gracious temper of his in verse 20–21: "Our conversation is in heaven, from whence we look for the Savior, the Lord Jesus Christ, who shall change our vile bodies and make them like to His glorious body." Let us from thence draw this inference: If we look that Christ should once at last vindicate our bodies from the dust, let us be ambitious to vindicate His gospel from the dirt. Do we look and hope that he will redeem our vile bodies from the grave? Then let us labor to recover His precious gospel from its tomb, and pray that at length it may have a glorious resurrection.

3. Let us consider how unworthily this glorious gospel has been defaced in our generation, and from

thence furnish our souls with matter for humiliation and lamentation. The primitive Christians are remarkable for all love; we may be justly reproached for all hatred. They were united; we are divided, subdivided, and crumbled into parties. Love and affection are now confined to some discriminating mode of profession; and the inquiry is not now whether a man bears the image and superscription of Christ, but whether he bears ours. The old heat of primitive zeal is turned into a feverish, preternatural heat against each other. It would be difficult to touch this point and not break out into satire. But we cannot reprove another without reproaching ourselves. We have been so fiercely biting one another that it is a miracle of divine mercy that we are not devoured by one another. Sheep, whose character has been meekness and mildness, have becoming roaring and ravenous lions. How little do we express the likeness of Christ who was meek and lowly in heart. The gospel would have taught us another spirit. "Forbearing one another, and forgiving one another, if any man have a quarrel against any, even as Christ forgave you, so also do ye" (Colossians 3:13:).

And we have added to that scandal which we have brought upon our holy religion, that we have entitled Christ to all our reproachful disorders; the argument runs now to divide and quarrel for Christ's sake, when it is for Christ's sake that we should unite and be at peace. Yet have we aggravated our guilt in a foolish thought to exonerate and justify ourselves by burdening and loading others, when the impartial can easily judge that all are wrong, but never determine who is in the right. Thus are we blindly falling upon one another, when every man should strike his hand upon his own heart, and cry out, "What have I done? Wherein have I contributed to that reproach and scorn that has been thrown upon our religion?" We are sharp-sighted to see the slips of our brethren, but blind to observe our own scandalous falls. And as the rain that falls upon the hills is discharged upon the valleys, the valleys again empty themselves into the rivers, and the rivers throw all into the sea, thus are we discharging ourselves and charging our brethren, who with equal zeal and passion, and perhaps with equal justice and reason, are retorting the same crimes upon us. In the meantime, we are mutually throwing dirt in one another's faces, tossing firebrands at one another's heads, and thereby setting all in a flame that may involve us all, our liberty and churches in the same common desolation.

Let us bitterly lament that any of the precious doctrines of the gospel have been so miserably abused, their gracious designs frustrated upon us, and perverted by us. For instance:

What more endearing truth is there than that of the patience of God waiting upon and striving with sinners to lead them to repentance (Romans 2:4)? And yet what doctrine is more impiously abused? God is long-suffering, and men will be long sinning. God waits, and they will find work for His patience. "Thus He gave Jezebel space to repent, and she repented not" (Revelation 2:21). He affords day after day to repent in, and they turn them into days to be repented of. Like zealous gamesters who have but an inch of candle left, they will play it out; and if the light had lasted longer, they would have drawn out their sports longer, and gone to bed in the dark. Such are all impenitent sinners who, having a day of grace, an hour of mercy, or a moment

of life wherein to turn to God, sport away those precious hours and moments not lent to them for those
ends. And if life were prolonged a thousand years, if
their days were eternal, their provocations would be
eternal. And thus that goodness of God, which should
mollify their hearts, instead hardens them; and they
will be worse and worse because God is better. As if it
were not enough to be evil, though God is good, they
will be therefore evil *because* God is good. But this
treatment of the divine patience has been foretold in
2 Peter 3:3–4: "There shall come in the last days
scoffers, walking after their own lusts, and saying,
'Where is the promise of His coming? For since the fathers fell asleep, all things continue as they were from
the beginning of the creation. Where is the promise?' "
A promise indeed it is, a most gracious one to them
who wait and prepare for His coming, but a threatening, a most dreadful threatening to them who harden
their hearts by it. Impenitence turns a promise into a
threat. But upon what presumptions do they thus
harden their hearts? "Because all things continue as
they were from the beginning of the creation." Oh, a
most perverse gloss upon the text of divine forbearance! For verse 9: "The Lord is not slack concerning
His promise, as some men count slackness, but is long-
suffering to usward, not willing that any should perish,
but that all should come to repentance."

And what more comfortable doctrine is there than
that of the free pardon of sin and justification through
faith in the righteousness of Christ? Romans 3:24:
"Being justified freely by His grace, through the
redemption that is in Jesus Christ." We cannot mention
without bitter tears that men will therefore freely sin

because God will freely pardon. If His grace abounds, they will abound in ungraciousness. His mercies are great, and they will therefore provide great sins to employ and exercise His great mercy. What a poisonous heart must that be that converts (or rather perverts) so sweet a doctrine into mortal poison?

Nor has it fared better with the doctrine of the perseverance of saints, which has not been cried down only by such as deny it, but reproached by those who own it. The gospel would teach us to work out our salvation with fear and trembling because it is God who works in us to will and to do of His own good pleasure (Philippians 2:12). We are not to be slothful because God works, but to work more diligently because we have the divine assistance. The same gospel would engage us (2 Peter 1:10) to make our calling and election sure. We are to make sure that we are effectually brought home to God, and from thence to infer our election, and not to delude our souls with the sophistry of hell that says, "If I am elect I shall be saved, though I wallow in all manner of abominable filthiness."

Let us renew our lamentations that the lives of professors express no more of the power of the truths and precepts of that gospel which they profess. The temper of religion as described in the Scripture is meekness, humility, compassion, beneficence, charity, and heavenly-mindedness; but these are so ill copied by those who profess Christ that we may seek for religion among those who are religious and not find it. And by this means Christ Himself is represented as unlovely and undesirable, and the inward enmity in the hearts of men is provoked, exasperated, and inflamed in persecution.

And from hence it is that wicked men think they have sufficient matter to justify all their revilings and blasphemies against our Savior and His doctrine, and think they do God service while they are endeavoring to root out of the earth a religion which is rendered odious by the unsuitable conversations of those who seem to glory in it. The offenses that are given will not justify those who take them. There is a woe denounced against the world because of offenses, and there is a woe denounced against those who give them. Matthew 18:7: "Woe be to the world because of offenses, for it must needs be that offenses come, but woe unto them by whom the offense cometh." Thus they who take the offense fall into hell, and justice sends him there who gave it.

USE OF EXHORTATION. I conclude with a word of exhortation. To all you who profess the doctrine of God and Savior, the doctrine which is according to godliness; and yet have seen it lie gasping, bleeding, and ready to die, oh, pity a holy doctrine that suffers unworthy things, and a Savior who suffers with it. When you lay in your blood, the divine pity that saw you wallowing there hopeless and helpless said unto you, even when you were in your blood, live (see Ezekiel 16:4–6)! And have you no compassion for a bleeding Jesus? It was enough that He once suffered for you; let Him not a second time be crucified and murdered by you! When the Spirit of grace shall be poured out that is promised in Zechariah 12:10: "To make us look upon Him that we have pierced"; there will be bitter mourning, as that for an only son, for a first born, for the untimely death of a good Josiah in the valley of Megiddo—let none of us say, "What is all this to us? Let them see to it who were guilty. Let Judas look to it who betrayed and sold Him; let Pilate look to that who condemned Him; let Herod look to that who buffeted and scourged Him; let the bloody soldier look to that who pierced His side with his spear. But as for us, we are innocent, and can wash our hands in innocency with Pilate, saying we are innocent of the blood of this just Person!" Oh, wretched evasions of deceitful hearts! We, even we in this professing age, this generation of professors has pierced and crucified the Lord Jesus. As it will be charged upon some at the great and dreadful day that the kindness they might have shown, and did not show to His brethren, was not shown to Him, so will it be charged that the dishonor, the scandals, and the reproaches they brought upon His doctrine, His truths, and His worship was thrown upon His person.

I have heard of an aged gentlewoman who, having an only son who it seems had found a pistol in some secret place of the house, she presented it to his breast in pleasantry, but the pistol fired and shot him in the heart. He had only so much time and strength as to say, "Ah, mother! You have slain your only son!" Think with yourselves what amazement, what confusion, what consternation seized her soul when the heart's blood of a dutiful son, of an only son, spun out into her face, his dying accents sounded in her ears, and she found herself childless in one moment through her own rashness and folly!

Let us set before our eyes the blessed gospel of our dear Lord Jesus, wounded, bleeding, and dying by our careless walkings, by our animosities and heats which have boiled up into hatred! Not only His seamless coat, but His tender heart is rent in pieces by our divisions,

together with the triumphs of the profane, who insult
religion and say, "Down with it, down with it, even to
the ground." And now it is fallen, and shall rise up no
more. Look seriously upon these things, and then tell
me, tell your own souls, and let an awakened, wounded,
and reflecting conscience tell you, with what regret,
with what self-abhorrence, you, we, all of us should re-
sent these indignities offered to the dear and precious
concerns of our God and Savior.

I am assured, and rejoice in that assurance, that
there is a sound part among the professors of the
gospel which has not drawn this condemnation upon
their own heads. There was one Joseph among the
guilty Sanhedrin who had not consented to their unjust
sentence (Luke 23:51). There are holy souls who mourn
in secret for all the abominations that be done in the
midst of us (Ezekiel 9:4). And there may be others
whose hearts God has touched with sorrow for the sins
of others, and repentance for their own. Now, for the
sake of these, and such others as the convincing grace
of God shall reach, I will give some counsel and advice,
and offer some motives to give an edge to that advice.

9

Counsel and Advice

There are things we must avoid if we sincerely design or ever hope to recover the credit of the doctrine of the gospel:

1. We must watch against the breakings out of ungovernable passions. A passionate man's heart is like gunpowder: it may lie quiet and still at present, but the least spark of a provocation sets it all ablaze. Or it is like the fluids in the body which are calm and sedate, but they only wait for an occasion to set them into a ferment. Once we lay the reins upon the necks of our passion, the inferior part runs away with the superior; that is, the beast rides the man, runs away with him, perhaps throws him, and breaks his neck. In these paroxysms, reason and religion are dethroned, and a base lust usurps the place.

He who will not keep a severe hand upon and over these unruly passions lies open to the assaults and practices of the devil. Proverbs 25:28: "He that hath no rule over his own spirit is like a city that is broken down, and without walls." When the walls are demolished, the strength is gone, and we become an easy prey to our enemy, and even tempt the tempter to invade us. It is meekness, humility, and patience that give us and keep us in possession of our own souls (Luke 21:19).

Now consider what mischief this passion has done to religion: Our differences were but few until passion

multiplied them, inconsiderable until passion height-
ened and greatened them. We have no controversies
but might have been fairly buried in Christ's grave. He
who could compromise the differences between a justly
provoked God and unjustly provoking men might be
supposed able to compose those between brethren; but
pride and passion have inflamed the reckonings, and
who now is able to quench the flame?

As others who behold our passions will suspect all is
not right with us, so have we most reason to suspect
ourselves, and to question whether the Word of God
has ever taken any saving hold of our hearts when it
cannot govern the intemperance of our lips. James 1:26:
"If any man seem to be religious, and bridleth not his
tongue, that man's religion is vain." It is in vain as to
any acceptance it finds with God, and in vain as to any
satisfaction it can give the conscience. And thus the
fiery professor tempts all the world to judge there's no
religion in him, and then to conclude that there is as
little in religion. This frightens outsiders from the
good ways of God; they render religion so unlovely, so
uncomely, and so little amiable that strangers think it
better to be as and where they are than to become
Christians, some of whom they see more fit for bedlam
than the church.

If we could learn to discern the divine providence in
men's provocations—and that as the evil one has a
hand in them, the righteous God has an overruling
hand in them too—it would serve to dash the ferment
of our most boiling passions and teach us to say with
the psalmist, "The Lord has bidden him to curse me."
The sense and fear of God vigorous upon our hearts
would fortify them against the sudden eruptions of

these distempers. Proverbs 23:17: "My son, be thou in the fear of the Lord all the day long, and let not thy heart envy sinners."

In a word, it would abate our passion, and the pride that feeds it, did we but calmly consider that our strongest passions are our greatest impotencies, and that while we indulge this we merely make work for repentance. What a folly it is to give way to that which must cost us bitter tears and sorrow before we can heal those wounds which thereby we have given both our own consciences and our profession.

2. Avoid all fraud, falsehood, and overreaching in your covenants, contracts, and dealings with your neighbors. Every Christian, besides that business he has with his God and his own soul, has affairs in this world. In all these, let your heart be true to God, your tongue true to your heart, and your heart and tongue both true to your neighbors. Ephesians 4:25: "Wherefore putting away all lying, speak every man the truth with his neighbor; for we are all members one of another." We are all members either in the first Adam or in the second; if in the first Adam only, yet why should we defraud our own flesh and blood? If in the second, why should we wrong them who are with us in the same Spirit (1 Corinthians 6:17)?

The psalmist, in Psalm 15:1, propounds this great question, and propounds it to God Himself, who alone could answer it: "Lord, who shall abide in Thy tabernacle? And who shall dwell in thy holy hill?" Who is that blessed man whom God will admit to communion with His blessed self in grace and glory? Among other characteristicss that describe this person, verse 2 gives this one: "He that walketh uprightly, and worketh righ-

teousness, that speaketh the truth in his heart." Verse 4:
"He that sweareth to his own hurt and changeth not."
Let others go beyond him in temporal matterss, he will
be true to his own soul, to his God, to his neighbor,
and to the credit of his religion. It is a great contradiction to religion to use falsehood in our commerces and
converses. Our God is the God of truth. His Word is the
Scripture of truth. In all that gospel which we preach,
there's not one proposition but what is truth. The apostle, in 2 Corinthians 1:18–19, purges himself of all levity
and inconstancy in his promises by the truth of that
gospel which he preached. "As God is true, our word
toward you was not yea and nay." It was not yea in
promising and nay in performing; for the Son of God,
Jesus Christ, was not yea and nay. Every yea of Christ is
yea; and every nay of Christ is nay. Fidelity therefore is
the image of God, and bears some strokes of His veracity; as unfaithfulness bears the image of the devil, who
is a liar and the father of it, and when he speaks a lie
speaks of his own (John 8:44). And if at any time he
speaks a truth, it is not of his own, but either by an overruling power extorted from him, or from some wicked
end of his own used by him.

3. Let us be jealous of and watchful over ourselves in
those things that lie near the flesh. Our corruptions
are like tinder: one spark struck into them sets all
aflame; whatever things therefore are most suitable to
those corruptions must be carefully inspected. Let us
watch over ourselves, watch against the tempter and his
temptations, and watch as those who watch for their
souls. Then pray that God would watch over us and all
our watchings, or else we wake and watch in vain.

The things that lie nearest our flesh are food and

raiment, which are apt to awaken and draw out sleeping corruptions. We read of some (Jude 12) who feed themselves without fear. Surely they do not know what an enemy they have lying in wait to surprise them. Holy fear would suggest these thoughts: "How do I know but that the tempter has laid a baited snare for me at my table? And when he is adorning the body, how do I know but that I may be now preparing a bait for another's soul?" Let every man study his own weak point; there the devil will be sure to assault you.

It was a dreadful, prophetic curse which the psalmist uttered against some in Psalm 69:22: "Let their table be made a snare; and let that which should be for their good be to their hurt." How sad it is to find death in the cup or dish where a man seeks his life. And yet how many eat and drink their own damnation, perhaps at Christ's table, and at their own! The wise man, or rather the wise God, has given us this counsel in Proverbs 23:1–2: "When thou sittest to eat with a ruler, consider diligently what is set before thee; and put a knife to thy throat if thou be a man given to appetite."

These thoughts would mortify the cravings of the flesh: After all our studious catering and carving for the flesh, yet we must die, and are now dying. While we are eating and drinking, perhaps while sinning, we are still dying. The means of life will not always prove effectual to preserve life. They who fed upon angels' food yet died (John 6:49:). "Meat for the belly, and the belly for meats, but God will destroy both it and them" (1 Corinthians 6:13).

It would greatly abate the luxury of the table to consider that the rich glutton, who fared sumptuously every day (Luke 16:19), was dead, buried, and in hell, where he could not by all his eloquent begging prevail for one drop of water to cool his tongue, scorched with those flames.

It might moderate our craving, wandering appetites to consider that nature is content with little, and grace with less; and whatever is beyond these comes of evil, and leads to evil.

If we cannot deny ourselves in the lesser instances, how will we deny ourselves in those more difficult trials which providence may possibly call us to? How shall we be able to lack necessary things when we cannot deny these extravagances?

What a reproach it is to a professor of religion to feel this raging hunger for the meat that perished when there is such a languishing affection for that which endures to eternal life! What a shame it is that we bring sharper stomachs to our own tables than to the Lord's.

I have hereby given you the advice of God as to what you must avoid if you would not defile.

10

Directions to Adorn the Gospel in All Things

I have given you the advice of God, what you must avoid if you would not defile. It remains now that I lay down those directions which you must observe if you will adorn the doctrine of our God and Savior in all things.

1. Severely govern yourselves, and the whole tenor of your conduct, by that royal law found in Matthew 7:12: "All things whatsoever ye would that men should do unto you, do ye even so unto them, for this is the law and the prophets." This is a law which Christ has transcribed out of the code of nature into His own, a law which once grew upon the stock of morality, but He has transplanted and inoculated into the gospel. Therefore the Apostle James (2:8) calls it a royal law: "If ye fulfill the royal law according to the Scripture, 'Thou shalt love thy neighbor as thyself,' ye do well." It is a law that carries the fairest stamp and signature of both the divine nature and authority, a law that shines with its own light into the soul of man. No man would defraud, oppress, or persecute another if he would give his conscience leave to put this question to himself: "Would I be thus treated, thus dealt with myself?" A due attendance to this rule would not only teach us to do justice, but to show mercy to others upon this single consideration: I expect justice, and may need mercy and pity from others. For certainly I am obliged to give what I expect,

and to show what I myself may need. Nothing would
more reclaim men from their unchristian, antichris-
tian barbarities than for us to put ourselves into the
same condition and case; to suppose ourselves chained
in the same prison, laboring under the same pressures,
with others of our brethren.

Whatever mercy, pity, or charity we may possibly
need in our extremity, let us learn to show it to others
in theirs. If we shut up our bowels of compassion, what
may we expect but that God will shut up His; and that
will restrain the bowels of compassion of all the world
to us. As the First Cause either draws nigh to us or re-
cedes from, so will the second either assist or forsake
us. The apostle offers this reason in Hebrews 13:3 why
we should remember those who are in bonds, and sym-
pathize with them, as if we were bound with them; and
them who suffer affliction, as being yourselves also in
the body. Suppose we are not actually bound, yet we are
in the body, and may be so. We are not sick as others
are, yet we are in the body, and may be so, and shall
then need those charitable visits, that relief, which we
now forget or neglect to administer. Or perhaps we
now abound and dwell at ease, yet still we are in the
body, and may soon in that very kind need compassion.

This may seasonably lead us into the admiration of
the pity, compassion, and bounty of our gracious God,
who, being out of the reach of our necessities, yet can
exercise tender mercy to us poor, sinning, and suffering worms; and into the admiration of the pities of
Christ, who now upon the throne, and out of the way of
those afflictions and temptations wherewith we are en-
compassed, yet has not left the human nature behind
Him, but has taken it with Him into heaven that He

might therein be compassionate to His distressed members, whom He is not ashamed to call His brethren (Hebrews 2:11).

This ought to teach us to do that justice to others which we expect others should do to us; for with what judgment we judge, we shall be judged (Matthew 7:2). This one thing would marvelously adorn the gospel, when we can convince all the world that our religion has made us better men when it made us Christians, and that we brought along with us morality when we espoused and came over to Christianity.

2. Maintain a heavenly mind and conversation. Let all see that, though your roots are in heaven, yet you bring forth fruit here on earth. It has reflected poorly upon our profession that we believe well, but live ill; we have a system of heavenly truths in our mouths, but we disparage them with earthly lives. A heavenly mind and a heavenly frame of heart would support a heavenly conversation.

Now because this is that great thing that must recover the credit and honor of the gospel, I will in a few words show you what it is:

• A heavenly mind is unmovably fixed and pitched upon heaven for its great and commanding end. This is his Father's house, to where he is always traveling; it is the port for which he is bound. And because there may be a mistake in the notion of heaven, as that it may be only a place of ease or a state of rest from the troubles of this life, he is satisfied that the enjoyment of God in that place makes the real heaven. Psalm 73:25: "Whom have I in heaven but Thee?"

• The heavenly mind and heart is always vigorously pursuing that great design; and because there are many impertinent avocations that would seduce or steal his heart from this end, he shakes them off with indignation, as those that would divert him in that holy pursuit. Nor does he so much consider how much of his race he has run, as he ties up himself to run the rest. Philippians 3:13: "Forgetting the things that are behind, and looking unto those that are before, I press towards the mark for the prize of our high calling in Christ Jesus."

• The heavenly mind endeavors especially to maintain a heavenly temper and frame of heart, which is the life of all heavenly pursuits. The habits of grace must be reduced into act and exercise; and grace must be laid out to its highest and noblest end. As the best instrument must be in tune before the skillful hand can make melody upon it, so must the heart be kept in a frame suitable to the services which are proper to it.

• A heavenly mind must conform itself to and exercise itself in those employments here below which are the proper work of heaven, always recovering itself when it deviates from its main end with this question: "My soul! How do the angels and the spirits of just men made perfect spend their blessed eternity above?" They are surely praising, blessing, admiring, adoring, loving, and serving their God, their Redeemer, their Sanctifier and Comforter; and why do not we conform ourselves to their pattern? The great law of heaven governs them, and every thought and motion of their wills; why do we not then more fervently pray that we may do the will of God on earth as it is done in heaven with the same cheerfulness and perseverance? And though we come short of their perfect love, praise, and service, yet let us be practicing and tuning our hearts and harps for those "hallelujahs." The work of eternity must be begun in time upon us, and done in time by us; nor is there a wilder fancy that can delude the vain heart of man than to imagine we shall leap at once from a life of murmuring and repining here to a state of praising and glorifying God forever.

We cannot doubt but such a life as this would put a new face upon the Christian religion, and convince the most obstinate that we suppose everlasting life and glory to be the most real, certain, and excellent thing, when we can live at the holy, heavenly, and cheerful rate which supposes it to be all these; that we firmly believe that whatever are the inconveniences of our pilgrimage, a portion in heaven will answer them and repay us. Therefore we look upon ourselves as dwelling in tents and tabernacles, without any fixed city here below, as those holy patriarchs once did (Hebrews 11:9), and we dare not drive our stakes too deep into the earth because we look long and pray every day to be called away home to our own country.

Let us study and follow after the things that make for peace. Our God is the God of peace; our Redeemer is the Prince of Peace; the Holy Ghost is the Spirit of peace; the gospel is a doctrine of peace, which revealed peace on earth, and good will towards men (Luke 2:14). But to our shame, and the shame of our profession, we have represented it as a civil war. We say we own one God, one Lord Jesus Christ, one holy Spirit, and one hope of salvation. Why then do we not keep the unity of the Spirit in the bond of peace (Ephesians 4:3–5)? Peace is that which everyone will commend, but very few will entertain. If we regard the orations of men, one would think it the most precious and desirable thing in the world; but if we observe their divisions, one would conclude it the most pernicious and dangerous. All differences in opinion do not infer a difference in religion, nor all local separations a schism; but when the smallest differences are managed by proud and froward spirits, and they are influenced by secular interests, it is a wonder to see what flames a little spark kindles. The sum is this: Perhaps we cannot syncretize in the minutes of religion, nor express the finer strokes of uniformity in our sentiments; yet let us religiously keep up a spirit of love to peace and truth. Christ has declared love to be the livery of His disciples, by which they are known to be His. John 13:35: "By this shall all men know that ye are My disciples, if ye have love one to another." As it was the livery He enjoined them while living, so was it His legacy bequeathed to them when dying. John 14:27: "Peace I leave with you, My peace I give unto you."

Let us all most fervently cry unto God that His Holy Spirit may be poured out upon the professors of religion, and that it may accompany the preaching of the gospel. Then will the doctrine of God our Savior shine gloriously, when the Spirit shall be its light; then will it conquer and triumph, when the Spirit shall second it with His might. This is that which subdues the pride, the passions, and the unruly lusts of men, and brings down whatever exalts itself against the truth in subjection to God. This influence attending the Word shall make persecutors become preachers; scoffers of religion shall become admirers of what they have scorned, and blasphemers will justify that name which they have reproached. This will give the doctrine of the gospel a throne in their hearts who have trampled it under their sordid feet. And this St. Paul well understood when he so earnestly entreated the churches' prayers in 2 Thessalonians 3:1: "Brethren, pray for us that the Word of the Lord may have free course and be glorified." When the light shall scatter the darkness that like a thick cloud sits upon men's minds; when the power of it shall bear down that opposition that rages in their hearts; when it shall break through all impediments and make its way to the conscience, then will the doctrine of our God and Savior adorn itself, and not need any other ornaments that we can put upon it.

I profess myself unwilling to dismiss this argument until it has had its proper effects upon the hearts and consciences of the readers; but I must draw to a conclusion, which I will do with a few considerations, humbly praying that the Great Lord and Master of the assemblies would drive every nail to the head, and so fasten it in the heart, so that the power and policy of the devil may never draw it out.

CONSIDERATION 1. What great reason have we to adorn the doctrine of our God and Savior, when we have been the cause or given the occasion to its dishonor. Justice demands that we should heal it because we have wounded it. I persuade myself that there are many under the rebukes of their own hearts that the name of our Lord Jesus Christ has been evil spoken of through their irregular conversations. I hope too that many have repented, and that God has pardoned the iniquity of their sin; yet God will bear a testimony against their careless and common behavior, though He has pardoned the sin. Thus He dealt with David in 2 Samuel 12:13–14: "The Lord hath put away thy sin, thou shalt not die. Nevertheless, because by this deed,

thou hast given great occasion to the enemies of the
Lord to blaspheme, the child that is born unto thee
shall die." In what way the jealous God will bear witness
against the present generation of professors for the
scandals they have given, I presume not to determine.
Most certain it is, He will not put up the affront without
repentance and reformation. The fastest course for
every one of us is to confess our sins, to take shame to
ourselves, to give glory to God, and not to blush at our
repentance, when the only thing should make us blush
is our sins.

CONSIDERATION 2. Adorning the gospel by a suitable conversation will prove the best expedient to secure its presence with us. If we think it is not worth
adorning, we may question whether God will think it
worth His continuing and protecting. It was disingen-
uous in Amnon to spurn his poor sister out of doors
when he had defiled her; but the justice of God will be
manifest if He removes our gospel which we have basely
prostituted. It is His own threatening to the church of
Ephesus in Revelation 2:5, "Remember from whence
thou art fallen and repent, or else I will come unto thee
quickly, and will remove thy candlestick out of its place,
except thou repent." A father takes away the children's
bread when they crumble it in scorn upon the ground.

Let us consult the histories of ancient times. They
will inform us that religion was never rooted out by
persecution until it had been made cheap by the profa-
nation of professors. The primitive Christians proved
that religion flourished fairer and grew faster when it
was watered with the blood of the martyrs. Prosperity,
and that looseness which commonly attends it, was the
poison poured out into the church. The frequent mow-

ing down of Christ's field makes it come up thicker and greener. Tertullian's observation was that debauching prosperity has been the greatest enemy that religion ever had in the world. In Isaiah 5:5, when God looked, as after all His cost and pains He might well look, that His vineyard should bring forth grapes, and it brought forth wild grapes. "Go to now, I'll tell you what I will do to My vineyard; I will take away the hedge thereof, and it shall be eaten up, and break down the wall thereof, and it shall be trodden down, and I will lay it waste."

The politics of earth are vastly different from those of heaven, in both the securing and the adorning of religion. The methods of human wisdom to secure religion proceed thus: They hedge it about with strict laws and severe penalties, which sometimes are as cruel as the crimes they would restrain are enormous. And while by these artifices they would entail religion upon posterity, corruption of doctrine, defiling of worship, and looseness of manners provoke God to cut off the entail. And thus, when we have lost the power of religion upon our hearts and the purity of it in our lives, our care is to supply the defect by trimming and tricking it up with gaudy ceremonial ornaments. How much more beautiful were our first parents in their original nakedness than when the sense of sin and shame taught them to patch together a few fig leaves to cover it? But religion is its own strength, its own beauty. It is its own ornament and fortress; nothing adorns, nothing secures religion, but religion. Let us therefore show an exemplary conversation, and this will beautify and fortify it better than all our political contrivances and fruitful inventions.

It was a glorious promise which God gave to the church under the notion of Jerusalem. Zechariah 2:4–5: "Jerusalem shall be inhabited as towns without walls and bulwarks. For I, saith the Lord, will be a wall of fire round about her, and will be the glory in the midst of her." Holiness engages God's special presence, and that presence is our protection. Secure God's glory in the center, and we shall have a wall of fire in the circumference. A parallel promise we have in Isaiah 4:5: "Upon all the glory there shall be a defense." If therefore we are careless of that glory, let us make what walls we can, our walls of water and of wood will deceive us; nothing but such a holiness as will engage the divine presence and protection can secure us, and the gospel of God our Savior unto us.

CONSIDERATION 3. Nothing but a holy, exemplary conversation can possibly propagate the gospel abroad. Our lives speak louder than our words, and we may with more ease "live" men over than dispute them over to Christ. Let us be never so zealous in our arguings, they will readily retort it upon us, "Why do you persuade us to go to Zion when you yourselves are running to Babylon?" In vain did we plead with others to turn and look towards heaven, if we are treading the broad way that leads towards hell. Do we then, indeed, wish well to the kingdom of Christ? Would we rejoice to see the heathen given to Him for His inheritance, and the uttermost parts of the earth for His possessions? First, remove the stumbling blocks we have laid in the way of their conversion, then win them over by a heavenly, holy, sober, and righteous conversation. Speak so that men may see that what you speak you believe to be the truth.

There were more brought in and converted in the first twenty years of the reformation than in the last century; and of our few modern converts (it is to be feared) need conversion.

This was the glory of the early days of Christianity. Acts 2:46–47: "They continued daily with one accord in the temple, and breaking bread from house to house, did eat their meat with gladness and singleness of heart, praising God. And the Lord added daily to the church such as should be saved." The same success the gospel had upon the same reason. Acts 9:31: "Then had the churches rest, and were edified, and walking in the fear of the Lord, and the comforts of the Holy Ghost were multiplied."

CONSIDERATION 4. The adorning of the gospel by a holy practical conversation would contribute much to the healing of our present deplorable divisions, our scandalous separations, and that spirit of frowardness and perverseness which has possessed this present generation. The differences among us are not so great as are imagined, nor yet so small as not to be lamented. Wisdom, humility, and a temper of moderation might have managed as great matters as these came to without any notable scandal. But a spirit of pride, hatred, and uncharitable censoriousness has inflamed these little things to a prodigious height.

Now the process was thus: some professors had given offense by their remiss, or perhaps some irregular walking; there began the offense, first at the person, then at the profession. The disgust at one grew up to a disgust against all of the same denomination. From an offense at the persons, it grew into a distaste of their worship and administrations. And when this dividing zeal had usurped the title of divine fervor, then heaven and earth, church and state, must be involved in unquenchable flames. This was therefore the generous spirit of the apostle in 2 Corinthians 11:12: "What I do, that I will do, that I may cut off occasion from them which desire occasion, that wherein they glory, they may be found even as we."

But I must end this discourse, which a sincere desire to restore our holy religion to its due honor and reputation has made to grow under my hands to a bulk far greater than at first designed.

Give me leave to reassume my exhortation. I beseech you, brethren, by the mercies of God, and the mercies of our Lord and Savior, that you would consider and pity the sad case of His blessed gospel, which has been wounded either by our hands, or through our sides, and make it your great business to adorn it in all things. I do not deny that, though you should walk like angels, there are a generation of men who will reproach you as devils; yet there are many curable souls whose reconciliation to the ways of God lacks nothing, waits for nothing so much, as that you should show them the way to heaven by your heavenly example. And that our endeavors may be successful, let us all join with the prophet in his pious prayer found in Habakkuk 3:2: "O Lord, I have heard Thy speech and was afraid. O Lord, revive Thy work in the midst of the years, in the midst of the years make known; in wrath remember mercy." Amen.

Appendix

The Sinfulness of Strange Apparel

or

What distance ought we to keep in following the
strange fashions of apparel which come up
in the days wherein we live?

The Sinfulness of Strange Apparel

"It shall come to pass in the day of the Lord's sacrifice, that I will punish the princes, and the king's children, and all such as are clothed with strange apparel."

Zephaniah 1:8

That this prophecy was sychronal with the reign of good Josiah appears from verse 1. It was a heinous aggravation of Judah's sin that they were unreformed under a reforming prince. Of him it was said that "there was no king before him that turned to the Lord with all his heart, and with all his soul, and with all his might, according to the laws of Moses; neither after him arose there any like him" (2 Kings 23:25). Of them it may be said that there was no generation that turned from the Lord, that departed from the law of their God, before them; though afterwards there were those who equaled or exceeded their wickedness.

The prophet, therefore, without the solemnity of a preface, immediately proceeds to sentence: "I will utterly consume all things from off the land" (Zephaniah 1:2). How could more of wrath be expressed in fewer words? There is consumption, then utter consumption, and utter consumption of all things. Is that not the abstract and epitome of final and total desolation? To silence all objections that might be made against this righteous sentence of God, the Lord commands, "Hold thy peace at the presence of the Lord God; for the day of the Lord is at hand; for the Lord hath prepared a sacrifice, He hath invited His guests" (verse 7).

Judah was to be the sacrifice. They who will not offer a sacrifice of righteousness shall be made a sacrifice to justice. The armed Babylonians were to be the priests. And the rabble of their enemies were to be the hungry guests, who would not spare, but would glut themselves with the spoil of Judah to teach them (and us through them) that if God is not sanctified in the hearts of a people professing His name (Leviticus 10:3), He will be sanctified on their heads.

Now in this "day of the Lord's sacrifice," however the main of the storm and hurricane would fall on the heads of the idolaters, and those "that sware by the Lord and Malcham" (verse 5), upon all the apostates, and such as shook off the worship of God (verse 6), yet some drops of the storm, a skirt of the shower of vengeance, would light upon a sort of second-rate sinners: "such as were clothed with strange apparel." Or, if the sinners were the same, yet this sin would be cumulative, and, when the ephah is brim-full, one single drop more will make it run over.

In these words you may observe the criminals, the crime, and the punishment.

The criminals are either the principals ("the princes and the king's children), or, as the Septuagint renders it, the rulers and the king's household, that is, the magistrates, nobles, and judges of the land. As they were lifted up above the level of the common person, they ought to have gone before them in all examples of sobriety and gravity; whereas now their levity in what was decent and grave, and their affectation of what was novel and vain, had drawn the people into a participation of the same sin, and an inclination to the same punishment as themselves.

The accessories to the crime were "all such [of whatever order, rank, or degree they were] as were clothed with strange apparel." Whose sin was the greater, and whose punishment should be the heavier, is difficult to determine. For the grandees would plead that some latitude was to be indulged there in respect of their quality and character. And the inferior sort would argue that they only copied the example set for them by their betters. But we will leave them to quarrel and debate the point among themselves. Both are included in the same condemnation, and it may safely be referred to the divine justice to measure out vengeance in proportion to their respective aggravations.

The crime is to be "clothed in strange apparel." The words used by the Septuagint can denote two things. The first is "exotic and foreign apparel," such as they fetch far and have bought dear in the prince, and must pay much dearer for in the punishment when justice shall call them to a reckoning. The Jews are noted for being a people exceedingly fond, even to doting, over foreign vanities—foreign wives, foreign worship, and foreign gods too. We read that Ahaz chanced to spy an altar at Damascus that largely pleased him. God's altar at Jerusalem was a plan piece, but this was a rare specimen of art. So he sent "to Uriah the priest the fashion of the altar, and the pattern of it, according to all the workmanship thereof" (2 Kings 16:10). For if a prince has an itch to innovate in or make change to his religion, a priest will easily be found that shall justify it.

The words may also denote "such as they had newly invented among themselves," for they had fruitful, inventing heads (though barren hearts) which could conceive a vanity and bring forth a lie, as soon as the most sickly soul could long for it (Job 15:35).

This "strange apparel," whether native or foreign, might be so for the matter or the form. Light minds, constant in nothing but inconstancy, would always be varying either the stuff or the shape, the ground or the trimming; and it would have been as easy to make a coat for the moon as to have fitted the fickle humor of that unstable generation. And indeed, at last they had their "round tires like the moon" (Isaiah 3:18), the liveliest emblem of uncertain, desultory fancies that could have been invented.

The punishment is indefinitely expressed. "I will punish," but how, or in what way, degree, or measure He will punish, He keeps to Himself. As there is not a greater threatening than for God to promise an impenitent people that He will punish them, so it looks very angrily when God threatens to punish, but conceals the manner of the execution, as if it must be some "strange" punishment that God would invent for "strange apparel," or some curse not written in God's book that must fall on the heads of such a vertiginous and giddy people.

The crime, then, you have heard; the criminals you have seen; the punishment must be understood. In the meantime, from this text a fair occasion is offered to propose and answer this question.

So what distance ought we to keep in following the strange fashions of apparel which come up in the days wherein we live?

That the present generation is lamentably intoxicated with novelties, and is sadly degenerated from the gravity of some former ages, can neither be denied, concealed, defended, nor, I fear, reformed. And, what is more deplorable, some who wear the livery of a stricter profession are carried away with the vanity of it. Even the "daughters of Zion" have caught the epidemic infection (Isaiah 3:16). And this has made the question, though in reality of little consequence, to be of great importance. Before I can give a direct and distinct answer to the question proposed, I must crave your patience so that I may lay down these preliminary considerations.

1. It is exceedingly difficult to fix and determine the lowest degree of conformity to these new fashions (which is sinful), and the highest degree of conformity to them (that which is not sinful). That is because the decision of the point depends on many nice circumstances which must all be duly weighed. And if the scales are not exact and true, the hand that holds them steady, and the eye that judges clear, it will be impossible to form a judgment in the case.

2. Therefore Satan has the greater advantage to overreach us, and our own hearts to betray and deceive us, because it is easy to slide insensibly from the lawful to the unlawful when it is so hard to discern to a hair's breadth where the one ends and the other begins.

3. Pride will be sure to perplex and entangle the controversy. Seeing that a haughty heart will never confine its licentiousness to the narrow rule of God, it must widen the rule and stretch it to its own extravagances. That lust which scorns to bow its crooked practices to the straight rule will not fail to bend the rule, if possible, to its own crooked practices; for it is very uneasy to sit in the stocks of a man's own conscience.

4. There may be some danger, as well as much diffi-

culty, in the determination since the universality of the corruption, like a deluge, has overspread the face of the earth, and interest is taken into the confederacy, with whom to combat is an unequal contention. Pride and profit, glory and gain, have their distinct concerns in this controversy; and to decry the silver shrines of Diana, by which so many craftsmen get their livings, must raise a heavy outcry against the opponent (Acts 19:23–27). And when obtaining custom shall second and back these corruptions, he must have oak, or brass, with triple fold, around his daring bosom rolled, that is, a very hardy spirit that shall dare to cross the stream or stem the current of a prevailing luxury.

So that, to have a finger in this ungrateful debate must engage him in Ishmael's fate: to have every man's hand lifted up against him, seeing that it is unavoidable that his hand must be set almost against every man (Genesis 16:12).

5. Yet charity will lend us one safe rule, that we impose a more severe law on ourselves and allow a larger indulgence to others. The rule of our own conduct should be with the strictest, but that by which we censure others should be a little more with the largest. For thus has the apostle taught us to proceed in things which in their own nature are indifferent (Romans 14).

6. Prudence will also afford us another excellent rule: in dubious cases we ought to take the safer side; we ought not to venture too near the brink of a precipice when we have enough room to walk securely at a greater distance. For, seeing the best that can be said of and pleaded for many of our fashions is that in themselves they are adiaphorous, which yet in their common practice are sinful. It becomes a Christian to

be cautious, and practice only that which is confessedly innocent and inoffensive; for he who will always do what may lawfully be done shall sometimes do what is unlawful to be done.

7. A humble heart, crucified to the world, and making a conscience of its baptismal covenant whereby it stands engaged to renounce the pomps and vanities of a wicked world, with all its fomentations of and inclinations to the flesh, will be the best casuist. Mortification would cut up the controversy by the roots, cure the disease in the cause, and cleanse the stream in the fountain. Nor can any determine for another so well as he who is true to his soul might for himself.

8. Yet there are some modes of apparel which so notoriously cross the ends of all apparel, which are so inconsistent with the rule of decency, and so apparently transgress the bounds of modesty, that no pretense of an honest intention, no uprightness of heart, can atone for or excuse the evil of wearing them. For instance, if a garment was made of silk, wrought with such figures as imitated the pictures of Aretine, and represented nakedness in all the most obscene and filthy postures, the use of such raiment would be a gross abuse, and no internal chastity could alleviate the guilt of the outward modesty.

9. Though some modes of apparel can never be well used, there are none but may be ill used; not so good that they cannot become bad (though some are so bad that they can never be made good). The reason for the difference is because all circumstances must concur to render a practice lawful, when the want of any one which ought to be present is enough to render it sinful.

10. Though sumptuary laws may justly be made to re-

trench the excesses, yet none can be lawfully enacted to
compel men in the defects of apparel. A law may say,
"You shall go no farther," but it cannot say, "Thus far
shall you go." And the reason is that they who can
reach the standard assigned by the law may lawfully
abate at the command of authority when, perhaps,
some cannot reach the lowest pitch without
entrenching upon their purses or consciences.

Having premised these things, I repeat the question:
What distance ought we to keep in following the
strange fashions of apparel that come up in the days
wherein we live?

The resolution of this will depend, first, on an impartial inquiry wherein the sinfulness of apparel lies;
second, on some directions how to walk at a due distance from these strange fashions, so that we do not
partake of the sin that may be in them.

Let us then, first, inquire wherein the sinfulness of
apparel lies. That difficulty will be best discharged by a
further inquiry into these four questions:

QUESTION 1. For what ends does God appoint and
nature require apparel?

ANSWER. In the state of innocence and primitive
integrity, nakedness was man's richest clothing. No
ornament, no raiment, was ever so decent as then was
no ornament and no raiment. For as there was then no
irregular motion in the soul, so neither was there any
in the body that might dye the cheeks with a blush or
cover the face with shame. "They were both naked, the
man and his wife, and were not ashamed" (Genesis
2:25).

But once they had violated the covenant, and broken the law of their Creator, shame, the fruit and

daughter of sin, seized their souls, and that in respect of God and of each other. The best expedient that their confused and distracted thoughts could pitch upon was to stitch together a few fig leaves to make themselves aprons, till God, commiserating their wretched plight, provided better covering, more adequate to the necessity of nature, more comporting with decency, that is, "coats of skin" (Genesis 3:7, 21).

Wherein the divine wisdom so admirably contrived that their apparel might serve as a standing memorial of their demerits, that they might carry about them the continual conviction of their sin and its deserved punishment. For what less could they infer than that they deserved to die the death which the innocent beasts must die to preserve and accommodate their lives? Also, their apparel was to direct their weak faith to the promised Seed, in whom they might expect a better covering and from a greater shame, that of their filthiness in the sight of God; in Him, I say, whom those beasts, probably slain in sacrifice, typified. For that any were slain merely on the account of food before the flood is not probable, when yet the distinction between the clean and the unclean, on the account of sacrifice, is demonstrable (Genesis 7:2).

Now God appoints, and nature requires, apparel:

1. To hide shame and to cover nakedness. Clothing was given that our first parents and their posterity, in their exile from paradise, might not become a perpetual "covering of the eyes" and a shame to each other. So it follows that whatever apparel or fashions of apparel either cross or do not comply with this great design of God must be sinfully used. It also follows that as any apparel or fashions of apparel more or less cross or do

not comply with this end, they are proportionately more or less sinful.

But our semi-Evites, aware of danger from these conclusions to their naked breasts, will readily reply that this will be of no great use to decide this controversy because it is not clear what parts of the body God has appointed to cover. Nor is it clear which of them may be uncovered without shame, seeing that some parts, such as the hands, the face, and the feet may be naked without sin to ourselves or offense to others.

To this I answer that the use of the parts and their designed ends are to be considered in this case. The use of the face is chiefly to distinguish the male from the female and one person from another. The use of the hands is to be instruments for work, business, and all manual operations. To cover or muffle up those parts ordinarily, whose ends and use require them to be uncovered, is to cross God's ends and design, and so is sinful by consequence.

To uncover those parts promiscuously, and expose them ordinarily to open view for which there can be no such good ends and uses assigned is sinful. For the general law of God must always take place where the special use of a particular part does not require the contrary.

Therefore, all apparel or fashions of apparel which expose those parts to view, of which exposing neither God nor nature have assigned any use, is sinful. It is true, I confess, our first parents, in that hasty provision which they made for their shame, took care only for aprons. But God—who had adequate conceptions of their wants and what was necessary to supply them, of

the rule of decency and what would fully answer it—
provided coats for them so that the whole body (except
as before stated) might be covered and its shame concealed.

2. Another end of apparel was to defend the body
from the ordinary injuries of unseasonable seasons,
from the common inconveniences of labor and travel,
and from the emergent accidents that might befall
them in their pilgrimage. The fall of man introduced
excessive heat and cold spells. Adam and Eve were
driven out of Paradise, to wander and work in a wilderness that was now overgrown with briars, thorns, and
thistles, the early fruits of the late curse; and clothes
were assigned to them in this exigency for a kind of
defensive armor. Hence we read that "Saul armed David
with his own armor; and he armed him with a coat of
mail" (1 Samuel 17:38). In the Hebrew it reads, "Saul
clothed David with his clothes; and he clothed him
with a coat of mail." The word there used is nearly the
same as the one in my text translated "apparel."

So whatever modes of apparel do not comply with
this gracious end of God in defending our bodies from
those inconveniences are sinfully worn and used. It is a
horrid cruelty to our frail bodies to expose them to
those injuries against which God has provided a remedy, just to gratify pride or to humor our vanity. And
however people hope to keep themselves warm and
shelter their sin under the screen of their own foolish
proverb ("pride feels no cold"), yet God has oftentimes
made their sin to become their punishment while, by
an obstinate striving with the inconveniences of an ill-
contrived mode, they have hazarded, if not lost, their
health, if not their life, by a ridiculous yielding to some

new fashion. But how will they stand before the righteous judgment seat of God when He shall arraign and try them as being guilty of self-murder on the great day of scrutiny, they may well to advise and consider in a timely manner.

3. To these I may add that when God made man his first suit of apparel, He took measure of him by that employment which He had cut out for him. Man's assigned work was labor, not to eat the bread of idleness, but first to earn it by the sweat of his brow which, though at first it was a curse, is by grace converted into a blessing. And accordingly, God so adapted and accommodated his clothes to his body that they might not hinder readiness, expedition, industry, diligence, or perseverance in the works of his particular calling. Hence these things will be exceedingly plain:

(1) God, having appointed man to labor, cannot be supposed to have made any provision for, or given the least indulgence to, idleness. Intervals for rest to redintegrate the decayed spirits, cessation for a season from hard labor, God allows and nature requires; but exemption from a particular calling, or any dispensation for sloth in that calling, we do not find.

(2) God has suited clothing in all its forms and shapes to a person's body so that they do not prejudice him in the works of his particular calling. Whatever fashions of apparel are not suitable therein, and render him unfit or less fit to discharge the duties of it, are so far sinfully used.

(3) Therefore, they who, by unmerciful lacing, girding, bracing, or pinching themselves in uneasy garments can scarcely breathe, much less eat, and least of all labor, apparently offend this end of God's. And it

is just that they who will not, or create an impotency so
that they cannot, work should not eat nor breathe long
on the earth, whereof they are unprofitable burdens.

Plato calls the body "the prison of the soul," and
some have made their clothes the prison of the body,
wherein they are so cloistered, so immured in the cage
and ill ease of a pinching fashion, that the body is
made an unprofitable servant to the soul, and both of
them to God. But such pride has brought many to their
coffins.

4. There is yet another end of apparel, namely, the
adorning of the body. And in this all our wanton fash-
ionists take sanctuary. Out of that which I may force
them, or (so far as is sober and moderate) indulge
them, I shall first premise a few observations, and then
lay down some conclusions.

Let these few things be premised:

• Ornaments, strictly taken as distinct from useful
garments, do not come under the same appointment of
God as necessary clothing. For, first, it is ordinarily sinful to wear no apparel, but not so to wear no such ornaments. Second, the necessity of nature requires one,
but no necessity or end of nature requires the other.
God's ends, and nature's occasions, may be secured
and answered fully without these additional things.
Ornaments, then, are rather matters of indulgence
than precept; they are matters of permission rather
than injunction.

• Plain, simple apparel, as it is a real ornament to
the body, so it is a sufficient ornament to the body. For
if nakedness is our shame, apparel that hides it is so far
is beautifying and adorning matter. When therefore we
say that "God gave clothes for an ornament," we do not

say that He gave ornaments distinct from clothing.

• Ornaments are either natural or artificial. Natural ornaments are such as nature has provided, such as the hair given by God and nature to the woman to be her glory and her covering (1 Corinthians 11:15). Artificial ornaments are such as are the product of ingenuity and witty invention. In these, as God has not been liberal, so man has been very prodigal. Not content with primitive simplicity, he has sought out many inventions (Ecclesiastes 7:29).

• It is evident that God allowed the Jews the use of artificial ornaments as distinct from necessary apparel. "Aaron said unto the people, 'Break off the golden earrings, which are in the ears of your wives, of your sons, and of your daughters, and bring them unto me.' And when Moses saw that the people were naked (for Aaron had made them naked unto their shame among their enemies), then Moses stood. . ." (Exodus 32:2, 25). It seems, then, that to be stripped of their earrings was in some sense to be made naked, to be exposed to shame in the sight of their enemies.

• Yet there was some difference between the indulgence granted to the male and that to the female. Dr. [Thomas] Fuller observes this from the order and placing of the words "wives, sons, and daughters," intimating that those sons were in their minority, "under covert-parent," as he explains it in his work *Pisgah-Sight of Palestine*. This seems to be implied in Isaiah 61:10, where we find indeed the bridegrooms "ornaments," but only bride's "jewels," as if the masculine sex was restrained to a more manly and grave sort of ornaments, whereas females were allowed a greater degree of finery and gallantry. And when God permitted the Jewish women to borrow from their neighbors jewels of silver and gold, the use was not limited to their sons and daughters, and grown men were not considered (Exodus 3:22), which is also evidently inferred from Judges 8:24, where the army conquered by Gideon is said to have worn golden earrings, for they were Ishamaelites. This clearly implies that their golden earrings were an ornament peculiar to the Ishmaelites, and not common to the Israelites.

• Though there might be something typical or symbolic in the jewels worn by the Jewish women (as I conceive there was), yet the use of them was of common right to the females of their nations. Indeed, they were of ordinary use long before the Jewish polity was settled. "The man took a golden ear-ring of half a shekel weight [a quarter of an ounce] and two bracelets for her [Rebecca], hands of ten shekels weight [five ounces]" (Genesis 24:22).

These things premised, I will now lay down these conclusions:

Conclusion 1. Whatever pretends to ornament, which is inconsistent with modesty, gravity, and sobriety, and with whatever is according to godliness, is not ornament, but a defilement. Modesty teaches us not to expose those parts to view which no necessity, no good end or use, will justify; humility teaches us to avoid curiosity in decking a vile body which ere long must be a feast for worms; good husbandry will teach us not to lay out on the back what should feed the bellies of a poor family; and holiness will teach us not to keep such a stir about the outward man when the inward man is naked. Charity will teach us not to spend superfluously on your own carcass when so many of your Father's children lack

necessary food and raiment; and godly wisdom will
teach us not to trifle out those precious minutes
between the comb and the glass, between curling hair
and painting faces, which should be laid out on and for
eternity.

Let me recommend you read 1 Peter 3:2–4: "While
they behold your chaste conversation coupled with fear.
Whose adorning let it not be that outward adorning of
plaiting the hair, and of wearing of gold, or of putting
on of apparel; but let it be the hidden man of the heart,
in that which is not corruptible, even the ornament of
a meek and quiet spirit, which is in the sight of God of
great price." From this passage these things offer
themselves to your observation:

1. Plaiting the hair and wearing of gold, or golden
ornaments, are not simply in and of themselves condemned, but only so far as they are either our chief ornament, or as we are too curious, too costly, excessive,
or expensive in them. For otherwise, the putting on of
apparel, which is joined in the same thread and texture
of the discourse and sentence, would be condemned
also.

2. The rule for regulating these ornaments is that
they be visibly consistent with a chaste conversation. I
say visibly consistent; it must be such as chaste conversation as may be beheld: "While they *behold* your chaste
conversation." That pure vestal fire of chastity that
burns upon the altar of a holy heart must flame out and
shine in chastity of words, actions, clothing, and
adorning; for whenever God commands chastity, He
commands whatever may feed and nourish it, manifest
and declare it. And He forbids whatever may endanger
it, wound, weaken, blemish, or impair it.

3. Godly fear must be placed as a severe sentinel to keep strict guard over the heart so that nothing is admitted that may defile our own hearts, nothing steal out what may pollute another's. We must keep a watch over our own hearts and other men's eyes; neither lay a snare for the chastity of another, nor a bait for our own. This "chaste conversation" must be coupled with godly fear.

4. Holy fear and godly jealous will have enough work about the matter of ornament. We must not err in our judgment, as if these outward adornings with gold or plaited hair were of such grand concern, nor err in our practice, in an immoderate care and superfluous cost about them.

5. The rule must be that which Peter laid down as a pattern: "After this manner in the old time the holy women also, who trusted in God, adorned themselves" (verse 5). Note, first, that they must be holy women who are the standard of our imitation; not a painting Jezebel, nor a dancing Dinah, nor a flaunting Bernice, but a holy Sarah, a godly Rebecca, and a prudent Abigail. Second, they must be such as were "in the old time," when pride was pinfeathered, not such as now, since lust grew fledged and highflown; such examples as the old time afforded, when plain cleanliness was counted as abundant elegance; such as the world's infancy produced, not such as an old, decrepit age recommends to us. Third, they must be such as could trust in God to deliver them from evil because they did not rush themselves into temptation; for it is hardly conceivable how any could trust in God to give them victory who tempt and challenge the combat; or how any can expect that divine grace could secure them from being

overcome when they, by their enticing attire, provoke others to assail their chastity. If, then, "the daughters of Zion" will be the heirs of Abraham's faith, they must approve themselves the followers of Sarah's modesty.

Conclusion 2. Nothing can justly pretend to be a lawful ornament which takes away the distinction which God has put between the two sexes. That law given in Deuteronomy 22:5 is of moral equity and perpetual obligation: "The woman shall not wear that which pertaineth unto a man, neither shall a man put on a woman's garment; for all that do so are an abomination unto the Lord thy God." The Hebrew word translated "that which pertaineth" signifies any "vessel, instrument, utensil, garment, or ornament," military or civil, used for the discrimination of the sex, according to Henry Ainsworth in his *Annotations on the Pentateuch.* The Rabbis define it thusly: "The woman shall not poll her locks, nor put on a helmet or a tiara on her head; neither may a man put on a colored garment or golden jewels, where men do usually wear such jewels." God will therefore have the distinction between the sexes inviolably observed in the outward apparel. This is a fence around the moral law to prevent those murders, adulteries, and promiscuous lusts which, under those disguises would be more secretly and easily perpetrated.

Yet observe that there may be a case wherein, in some exigency, it may be lawful for the woman to wear the apparel of a man. Aterius says, "I knew a woman who cropped her hair and put a man's apparel so that she might not be distinguished from her dear husband, who was forced to hide and flee for his life."

What particular form of apparel shall distinguish the one sex from the other must be determined by the custom of particular countries, provided that those customs do not thwart some general law of God, the rule of decency, the ends of apparel, or the directions of Scripture.

Yet there seems to be some distinctive ornament provided by God so that the difference between the sexes might not be left to the arbitrary customs and desultory humors of men. An example would be the hair of the head and the manner of wearing it; or at least in the beard, which is ordinarily given to one sex and denied to the other. And hence it seems probably that for women to crop their hair, or for men to nourish it to full length, is a contravention to the discriminating badge and cognizance which the God of nature has bestowed upon them.

However, a prudent and cautious Christian will be well-advised how his practice contravenes the plain letter of a law when the distinctions used to avoid the dint and turn the edge of it are not very clear and satisfactory, but are instead precarious, and such as are contrived to ward off the force of an argument. An example is given to us by the apostle in 1 Corinthians 11:14–15: "Doth not even nature itself teach you that if a man have long hair, it is a shame unto him? But if a woman have long hair, it is a glory to her." The Greek words used for long hair on a man are literally "if a man wears his hair at the full length." Now the evasion used to escape the danger of this text is that by "nature" is meant no more than the custom of the country, which, being a second nature, is able to warrant whatever is conformable to it, as also to render whatever is opposite as indecent and uncomely. Since the custom of our country is altered, the sin is banished.

First, let it be considered that the phrase "even nature itself" seems to restrain the word to its proper and primary significance. Second, the apostle could not well argue against long hair, nourished to its utmost extent, from the custom of the Greeks, since they of all men are famous for wearing it hanging down. Homer notes this as the common epithet of the Grecians: "the Grecians that nourished their hair." Nor will it appear that they, from the Trojan War to the days of the apostle, had changed their custom, which they made much of as that which rendered them formidable to their enemies.

But supposing that custom alone had taught the men to wear their hair short, and women theirs at its utmost length, and that encroaching practice in process of time should introduce the customary custom— for men to cut their hair and men to nourish theirs— yet how many millions of sins must be committed before the new custom could prevail to jostle out the old practice and legitimate the new one! So they who plead this for themselves merely acquit themselves at the cost of other men's condemnation.

As the case stands with us, the custom is not so general, either for the number or quality of the persons (if by "quality" we understand those of a pious and religious character), as to justify the modern deviation from a generally-received practice. But I confess that if the commonness of the custom is not extensive enough to take away the sin, it is yet so prevailing that it has taken away the sense of it in the consciences of many professors.

Conclusion 3. Nothing ought to be allowed for ornament which crosses the end of all apparel, that of covering nakedness.

The Israelite women are said to have been "made naked unto their shame" (Exodus 32:25), when they were only deprived of their earrings, which were but one part of their apparel. But among us, our English ladies will not acknowledge it to be any nakedness, any shame to have their breasts exposed.

They will pretend that the parts which decency requires to be covered, and in whose nakedness shame lies, are only those which the apostle called "less honorable" or "uncomely" (1 Corinthians 12:23).

To this I answer, first, that no parts of the body are in themselves "less honorable" or "uncomely." Second, that the uncovering of any part will be so when no honorable use requires the uncovering. Thus the prophet calls the "uncovering of the locks, of the legs, the thigh" the "nakedness and shame of the Babylonians" (Isaiah 47:2–3), which, though it is meant of a necessitated nakedness—which may be a reproach, but not a sin—yet, when that is done voluntarily which then was done necessarily, it will become both the sin and the reproach.

It is pleaded that what they do is not out of pride (to glory in the beauty of the skin), nor out of lust (to inveigle others to become enamored at their beauty), but only to avoid the reproach of a morose singularity, and a little, perhaps, to comply with what has been the vogue among the more genteel and well-bred persons.

To remove this argument, first, it is a branch of holy singularity rather to be sober alone than mad for company. What Christian would not rather choose to lag behind than strain himself to keep pace with a hairbrained age in all its endless and irrational usages? And, second, compliance with a vain, humorsome gen-

eration is so far from being an excuse that it is an aggravation of the vanity of the practice.

But these are only the umbrages invented to palliate
the extravagance; the persuasive inducements lie much
deeper, which, because we cannot in all make a judgment of, we must leave them to the censures of their
own consciences. I dare not say that it is to allure or in-
vite customers, though what does the open shop and
sign at the door signify but that there is something for
sale? Nor shall I tax the practice of ambition to show
the fineness, clearness, and beauty of the skin; though,
if it were so, I would ask who are concerned, I pray, to
know what hue, what color it is of, but either their lawful husbands or their unlawful paramours? In the
meantime, it is all too plain that arrogance and impudence have usurped the place and produced the effect
of primitive simplicity. Women are now almost naked,
but are not at all ashamed.

*Conclusion 4. Whatever pretends to be an ornament, which
obscures that natural ornament which God has bestowed is not an
ornament, but a defilement.* The harmony and symmetry of
the parts each to the other, made and posited conveniently and proportionately to their proper ends and
respective uses, is the real beauty of the outward man.
Upon the front of the body is engraven in capital let-
ters: "GOD MADE." God is not ashamed of it, and neither should be; but neither should we be a shame *to* it.
The throne of this beauty is the countenance, which it
is the will of God should ordinarily be uncovered so
that the Workman may be seen in His workmanship.
And yet this frontispiece, this portal of the fabric,
which shows so much of divine art, God will have covered when exposing it to view exposes the soul to temp-

tation. God would have us turn away our own eyes from beholding vanity, and has provided a nimble covering so that with one twinkle we may prevent a dart shot at us out of the devil's bow, by whatever hand or from whatever quiver. And so He would have us turn away the eyes of others too when they may wound themselves and suck poison from the flower of loveliness and beauty.

Now if God would have the face covered, whose great end requires the open view, when uncovering it would do harm, how much more would he have the breasts covered whose uncovering may do harm, but can do no good, having no lawful end or use assigned for such laying open! And if God would have the face, the seat of beauty, to be visible, what shall we say of those who disfigure it by painting it so as discolor it. Now we may seek God in His workmanship, and His workmanship in the face, and find neither!

How would these wantons have repined at their creation, and perhaps blasphemed their Creator, had He made them as they have marred themselves! They would not doubt have gotten a room in the chronicles among the prodigious and monstrous births had they been born with moons, stars, crosses, or lozenges on their cheeks!

But here I shall answer some questions.

QUESTION. Is it not lawful to conceal a gross deformity?

ANSWER 1. Yes, no doubt, but not a natural deformity with an artificial vanity. He who gave you ordinary clothing expects that you will use it to hide your blemishes. But will nothing serve your turn but a fantastic vanity?

ANSWER 2. It is lawful to hide a deformity, but not with a greater one than that which you would conceal. A black patch, in truth, is pretended to hide a blemish, either natural or, it may be, accidentally contracted. Well, be it so. I demand, then, what if God had branded your cheek or stigmatized your forehead with a scar of the same figure and color with that which you have invented to hide what you now have? Would not such a mark have been accounted a greater blemish than what you now complain of? Why, then, do you, vain woman, hide a blemish with a deformity? All the quarrel, I perceive, which you have against the natural is that it was of God's making, and all the fancy which you have for the artificial is because it was of your own.

ANSWER 3. Much less is it lawful to hide a natural beauty with an artificial deformity; for what is this but to be ashamed of what God has done exceedingly well, and then to glory in what you have made a thousand times worse?

QUESTION. Is it now lawful to conciliate beauty where it is not, or to increase it where it already is?

ANSWER 1. A humble submission to the divine good pleasure is the best remedy for imaginary or real defects. Has God made any of us vessels of coarser earth? Who shall say to the Potter, "Why hast Thou made me thus?" (Romans 9:20). The best covering for the defects of the face is to lay our hand upon our mouth, and our mouth in the dust, and to be "dumb with silence" because "the Lord hath done it" (Psalm 39:9). "Where then dost thou contend with Him, who giveth not account of any of His matters"? (Job 33:13).

ANSWER 2. True grace is the most excellent receipt for beautifying your face. "Wisdom maketh the face to shine" (Ecclesiastes 8:1). There is something (though hard to say what it is) in an unaffected gravity, an unforced modesty, in an ingenuous, affable deportment, free and natural, without starch and pedantry, that recommends and endears more to the acceptance of the judicious than all of the curious mixtures of artificial, fading colors.

ANSWER 3. Perhaps the evil of your supposed defect and shortcoming is more in fancy than in reality. You are well enough if only you could think so. When we consider our moral blemishes, we deceive ourselves that we are good because we are not as bad as the worst; but when we reflect on our natural defects, we are apt to repine because we are not as good as the best. And when we pore over only what we lack, we lose the contentment, and our God the glory, of what we have.

ANSWER 4. And it should be considered that as some, designing to make it burn the clearer, snuff the candle too low, and so near that they quite extinguish it. As others are always careening the vessel of the body with medicine, washing and tallowing with eternal applications till they sink it, so many tamper continually to mend the features and complexion— which God made very well because it pleased Him to make them no other—till they utterly spoil them.

ANSWER 5. Yet we must know that there is a mid-sized beauty, a moderate rate of comeliness, which the ancients called mediocrity that is below envy and above contempt. Concerning this state I observe these things:

1. This moderate assize of beauty is the safest posture, and most secure from doing or receiving mischief from tempting or being tempted that we could be placed in. It is so in all outward concerns: the

cedar of Lebanon is exposed to storms; the thistle of Lebanon is liable to be trampled and trodden down by the insolent foot of every wild beast of the forest (2 Kings 14:9). And when we come to cast up our accounts in a dying day, or to give up our accounts in the last day, we shall find and acknowledge it to have been so.

2. It is lawful by natural means to recover what preternatural accidents have taken away. If sickness has impaired your complexion and beauty, health will restore it; let the physician do his part and restore health, and health will not fail to do her part and restore decayed comeliness better than the painter. That the physician is God's ordinance primarily to preserve life and restore health, I know; but whose the painter is when employed about the red integrating of faded beauty, you would best inquire of Jezebel, for I confess my ignorance.

3. It is not lawful to aspire after nor endeavor to procure the highest pitch of beauty that is attainable by art, when nature has denied it in things of greater value and nobler use than perishing complexion. God has set due bounds to our towering thoughts. I cannot conceive it lawful for me to desire Paul's gifts unless I have his employment; and we may possibly overshoot ourselves in begging for the highest measure of some graces unless what God calls me to shall require them.

4. Nor it is lawful to endeavor to restore by art what the ordinary course of time and age has deprived us of. It seems to me that we should acquiesce in the devastations which time has made upon our bodies, otherwise than as a rate of health suitable to that declining may make us more lively, active, cheerful, and vigorous in

God's work. "The hoary head is a crown of glory; and the beauty of old men is the gray head" (Proverbs 16:31 and 20:29). And are we ashamed of our glory? Do we despise our crown? Will nothing serve but juvenile hairs on an aged head? Must we try experiments to fetch back the spring in autumn? The former is indeed more pleasant, but the latter is more fruitful and profitable. Who would exchange the harvest for the seed time? Yet such is our frowardness that youthful wigs counterfeit black hair where age has made it gray. And thus, not seeking true glory in the way of righteousness, we affect and pursue a false, imaginary honor in a way of unrighteousness.

QUESTION 2. What is the true rule of decency in apparel?

ANSWER. That all indecent apparel is a transgression of the general rule ("Let all things be done decently and in order," or literally, "in a right scheme or in a decent habit") is easily granted; but to fix and settle the rule of decency will be a matter of greater difficulty, especially since much controversy has been raised about it on another and greater occasion. What influence it may have upon our main inquiry will appear from this confessed truth: the suitableness or unsuitableness, and by consequence the lawfulness or unlawfulness, of all apparel to the person who wears it will very much depend on its agreeing or disagreeing with this rule of decency.

There are six things which in conjunction will complete this rule: the outward condition, the age, the sex of the wearer, the climate, the law of the land, and the customs of the place where or under which

Providence has cast our habitation.

• The condition of the wearer in outward respects is of great consideration; for though all men are made of the same metal and materials by creation, yet all are not cast in the same mold by Providence. One wears a public character, another a private one. God has placed one on the throne while He has set millions to grind at the mill. Some are rich, others are poor; some are cut out to be masters, others are shaped only to be servants. And it seems to me that there should be some distinction in the outward habit proportionate to what Providence has made in the outward condition.

But to render this observation serviceable to the main design, take the following propositions:

Proposition 1. It is lawful, and in some respects necessary, that kings, princes, and magistrates, especially in the solemn exercise of their proper and respective offices, be distinguished by their robes from private persons, and from each other. All civilized nations have so unanimously concurred in this distinction that we may receive it as the dictate of nature, the vote of universal reason. Jehoshaphat wore his royal robes, though wearing them once would likely have cost him dearer than the matter and making of them (1 Kings 22:30–33). Solomon's outward glory was the admiration of the Queen of Sheba, and yet, when he shone in all his external luster and splendor, he "was not arrayed like the lilies of the field" (Matthew 6:29), which gloried only in the bravery of nature's own spinning. Just so short are the finest works of art of the coarsest manufactures and meanest pieces of the God of nature! And though Herod in his royal apparel was eaten by the worms, yet the sin did not lie in the richness of his robes, but in the rottenness of his heart.

Trying to be more than a man, he became less than a worm; and because he was ambitious of being a god, he did not have the civility usually given to men (Acts 12:21–23).

Proposition 2. There is a lawful difference of apparel arising from the difference of wealth, titles, and honors, though distinguished by no public office. Our Savior seems to approve of this in Matthew 11:8: "They that wear soft clothing are in kings' houses." Courtiers, then, may assume a garb somewhat above that of meaner persons, suitable to the glory of the prince on whom they attend. And our Lord and Savior in His practice justified some diversity, in that He used a more liberal diet and agreeable clothing than did John the Baptist, whose "raiment was of camel's hair, with a leather girdle about the loins; and his meat was locusts and wild honey" (Matthew 3:4). One garb was decent enough in the rude wilderness which would have been uncomely to Him whose habitation was mostly in the city.

Should I use as an example that rich man in Luke 16:19 who was "clothed in purple and fine linen, and fared deliciously every day," it would be answered that he was a riotous glutton, and that he deserves our indignation, not our imitation. And yet I might rejoin that his sin lay in pampering his carcass in the dining room while poor Lazarus could not get the scraps and crumbs that fell from the rich man's table. The truth is, it is a parable which always speaks a truth and is founded on a truth, the manner of teaching is artificial and feigned. Nor do I doubt but that our Savior modeled His parable by and calculated it for the innocent and allowed customs of His own country. Nor shall I make further use of that man who came into the assembly with his gold ring and goodly apparel (James 2:2), other than to observe that the sin lay neither in the one nor the other, but in the partial idolizing of a grandee merely on the account of his external attire, while the poor, good man was thrust down to the footstool, if not trampled under foot (James 2:3–4).

Proposition 3. No ability of the rich will warrant him in wearing any apparel inconsistent with the ends of God's appointment. The purse is no adequate measure of the lawfulness of apparel. Conscience may be straitened when the purse is enlarged. I note this for the sake of those who always defend themselves with a proverb which is as wicked as it dull: "If my mind wishes it, and my purse pays for it, what does anything else have to do with it?" I will tell you what does: First, nature, whom you have enfeebled; second, those souls that you have tempted; third, you yourself, whom you have defiled; and, last, God Himself, whose ends in giving apparel you have neglected and transgressed. Each of these have cause to bring action against you. A man, then, may be civilly able to follow fashion who is not morally able to do so. The purse may bear the charge when conscience cannot give you a discharge for your vanity.

Proposition 4. No measure of wealth can justify those garbs which speak pride or vainglory in the wearer. I grant that raiment may indicate no pride in one man who, out of his abundance, can spare the charge of it, which it would speak in another whose incompetent estate cannot reach the expense; and yet his ambitious mind affects the gallantry. Yet still pride and vainglory are abominable to God in the rich as well as in the poor, in the king as well as in the beggar. Difference of apparel may be allowed, but pride and vainglory cannot be tolerated.

Proposition 5. It is sinful to aspire after those costly garbs which are above our estates to maintain. A poor man may be as covetous of the rich, and ordinarily is more so because covetousness does not lie merely in the having, but in the immoderate and inordinate desiring to have what he does not have. And a mean man may be vainglorious and proud in his rags, and sometimes *of* his rags, because this humor does not lie so much in the wearing, as in the lusting to wear, glorious trappings beyond what his estate is able to support. And this I note for the sakes of those aspiring persons who, when they cannot for their lives reach the chargeable matter, yet show their goodwill to bravery by imitating the cheap vanity of the form and shape.

Proposition 6. Every man, in the account of God, clothes above his ability who withdraws from works of necessity, justice, and mercy to maintain his pride. No man is thought able to do a thing till he is able to do it when God and man have their own. The rich man's conveniences must be retrenched by the duties of justice and his superfluities by the acts of mercy; when these are subtracted out of the total sum of your income, the remainder is clearly your own (in the Lord).

There is a certain order of things which we must strictly observe. If food and raiment come into competition, the belly must carry it; food was before sin, raiment brought in by sin. If justice and mercy come into competition, justice must carry the day; we must pay what we owe, and then give what we can spare. If the necessities of another are competitors with me, my own must take place because I am bound to love my neighbor as myself, but not above myself. But if the necessity of a Christian stands in competition with my own superfluities, his exigency is to take place over my abundance; for no man is really able to be fine till he has paid all he owes to God and man, to creditors and petitioners.

• The age of the person will allow for some diversity of apparel. One thing may become little children playing in the marketplace with their fellows which would be ridiculous in the grave senator when he sits in the gates of the city. When we become men, it is hoped that we will put away childish things (1 Corinthians 13:11). Is it not nauseous to see a lady of eighty smug and spruced up as if she was in the flower of eighteen? They ought not to trim themselves as if they were newly coming in when they are just going out of the world! They ought not to harness themselves for a wedding when the coffin is being made, the grave is being dug, and the worms are preparing for them.

Inference 1. For aged persons by any habits or dresses to represent themselves as young and youthful is sinful. Their eyes tell them that they are old, but they do not believe it. Time has put gray hairs on their heads and they do not acknowledge it. Would they have others believe that they are what they would seem? Then they would have them believe a lie, which lie may be told by visible as well as audible signs. Or are they ashamed of their hoary head? Then they are ashamed of what God has made their glory. Do they hope to catch some young birds with that chaff? They are silly birds who are caught, but, in the meantime, how abominable is the cheater!

Inference 2. All youthful wigs and paintings, which are sinful in youth, are doubly sinful in the aged. Time has plowed deep furrows in the face, and they will fill them up with white and red. The clock of time has given warning for their last hour, and they try to set it back to noon. The sun is almost setting in the west, and they will outvie Joshua, not content that it should stand there for awhile, but would force it back to ten degrees on the dial of Ahaz (2 Kings 20:11).

• The sex may be allowed a share in the decision of this point, for the female has a greater latitude than the male. It was so with Israel of old, when the bride was allowed her jewels, but the bridegroom must rest content with an inferior sort of ornaments. It would be a culpable effeminacy for the man to affect and imitate all the lawful little ornaments of women.

Nevertheless, this indulgence is clogged with some humbling considerations:

Has God indulged females a fairer liberty? The very indulgence argues the sex's weakness. It speaks to her as being the weaker vessel because she needs it. They have small reason to glory in a privilege which is but a bade of their infirmity! As if a nobleman's servant should be exalted for his laced livery and silver cognizance, which is but the mark of a more honorable servitude!

Has God indulged females with a greater latitude? How it should then humble them that they have transgressed the boundaries of heaven's indulgence! God has given them a long rope, and must they break it? Will nothing serve, nothing satisfy, unless they range abroad in the boundless waste of their own capricious wills and fancies?

Know therefore that the same authority that has given the liberty has assigned due limits to it, which that they may be better understand, I shall open the words of the Apostle Paul: "I will that women adorn themselves in modest apparel, with shamefacedness and sobriety; not with broidered hair, or gold, or pearls, or costly array; but (which becometh women professing godliness) with good works" (1 Timothy 2:9–10). This is a divine glass wherein that sex may contemplate both their glory and their shame.

Here they may behold their real glory, which consists, first, in being adorned in "modest apparel," such that no steam, no smoke, no vapor or flame of immodesty without may reveal a latent fire of burning lust within. Theodoret says that "the very apparel should indicate the gravity of the soul." Jude 23: "Hating even the garment spotted by the flesh." A soul spotted with lust will stand the garment. Thephylact, speaking of ancient women, said, "They ought to appear modest by their very habit and clothing."

Second, their glory consists in being adorned with "shamefacedness." The face will bear a proportion to the heart, and the clothing to both. Rolling eyes, wandering looks, outstretched necks, seductive smiles, and evil glances disparage the most modest apparel. "The daughters of Zion," equivocally so called, were "haughty" in heart; and it soon appeared in the haughtiness of their necks (Isaiah 3:16). A humble soul will adorn its ornaments, while proud gestures and postures deform them.

Third, their glory consists in being adorned "with sobriety." Moderation of affection towards outward things is a Christian's holiday suit; we are not to overprize or overuse them. This temper should shine through all our garments.

Fourth, their glory consists in being adorned "with good works." And there is not doubt that had less been laid out on good clothes, more would have been spent on good works. But rich clothing has beggared charity; and since women choose to shine in their apparel, their light has shone less bright to the glorifying of their Father who is in heaven.

Fifth, here is the rule by which all is to be regulated: "as women professing godliness." Godliness must be our caterer and cook for the belly, godliness your tailor and seamstress for the back; godliness must be consulted as to what to buy, how to make up what you have bought, and how, when, and where to wear what you have made up. But did godliness advise you to paint or patch your face, to curl or crisp your hair? From what principles of godliness can these vanities proceed? By what rule of godliness are they ordered, or to what end of godliness are they designed?

In this gospel glass they may view their own shame, and they most of all glory in their curiosity and costliness. They glory in curiosity, doing much to no purpose, and doing all with great pains. "Plaiting the hair," or, as Peter phrases it, curling, crisping, twirling, variegating it into a thousand shapes, into rings, mats, shades, folds, towers, or locks (1 Peter 3:3). Tertullian inveighs bitterly against this sort of impertinence: "What ails you that you cannot let your poor hair alone? Some of you are all for curling it up into rings, others for a loose mode. Nay, not content with that, you stitch monstrous extravagances of false locks and artificial hair and wigs."

Oh, that I could give you a real prospect of a converted Mary Magdalene! She wiped our Savior's feet with the hairs of her head (Luke 7:38), as if she would take a holy revenge on that which had been the effects of her own pride and the cause of ensnaring others; as if she thought nothing too precious for Him who had rid her of seven devils; as if she had found more honorable employment for her locks than when they were woven into nets to catch poor, silly souls, decked with ribbons to be a lure to a gazing youth.

Second, they shame lies in the excessive cost of their ornaments, in "gold and pearl." Oh, the reproach that a little refined earth would be accounted the glory of the rational creature, that we should esteem that our treasure which came out of oyster shells, that we should be at such vast charge to pain a walking sepulcher, to embroider a tabernacle whose cords ere long must be cut asunder, whose stakes must be plucked up in awhile, and whose canvas covering must shortly be fretted into rags by the consuming moth!

In a word, God has given the woman some allowance. She who takes more forfeits all the rest. Look to it lest, while you adorn yourself with gold, God should call you "reprobate silver" (Jeremiah 6:30), and when you load yourselves with jewels, you are not found much too light in God's balance.

• The climate where we dwell may be of some consideration to fix the rules of decency. God has provided us wholesome cloth, and expects that we should cut our coat according to it. When the Sovereign Lord "appointed the nations the bounds of their habitations," He, as a careful Parent, provided suitably for all the inhabitants of the earth. Some He ordered to dwell under the equinoctial line, others under the polar circles. To the former He gave the silk worm so that, as they required less and lighter apparel, they might have answerable provision. To the latter He gave numerous flocks of sheep so that, as they needed more and warmer clothing, they might have it of their own growth.

But luxury has rummaged every corner of the earth to fetch home fuel to feed the insatiable fire of lust which, the more it eats, the more it hungers. Alexander Severus and Aurelianus, those great emperors, are reported never to have worn a garment of entire silk all their lives, which has become the ordinary wear of every nurse in a village. Emperors then were not clothed as fine as servants are now. It was more than 150 years after Christ that some idle monks brought into Europe these silk spinsters; and truly it is no great credit to the wear that they who first brought in strange religions and new fashions of worship should be the men who first introduced strange attire and new fashions of apparel. But so it is; while we pursue exotic, lying vanities, we forsake our own domestic mercies (Jonah 2:8).

• The laws of the land ought to carry a great stroke in the decision of what is decent. It were to be wished that evil manners might at length beget good laws. But we are not sick enough with this disease to feel the need for and submit to the prescription of state physicians. Such was once the extravagance of this nation in the prodigious breadth of their shoes, that they were restrained to six inches at the toes. Oh, monstrous excess, where the excess itself was accounted as moderation! But because I find no sumptuary laws in force at present, let us look a little back into former ages and step awhile into foreign countries.

The Lacedemonian *ephori* were exceedingly pointed on this matter. Æliani said, "A daily inspection should be made daily into the matters of apparel, that nothing

herein might vary from what was decent and of necessary comeliness." Suetonius, in *The Life of Julius Caesar*,
says that "Julius Caesar prohibited the use of purple or
scarlet and pearls, except to some certain persons of
such and such years." And Tacitus, the grave historian,
highly commends the prudence and policy of Caesar's
law, which "with admirable prudence, distinguished
the several ranks of citizens by their apparel; so that
they who were advanced above others in offices,
degrees, and honors, should also be differenced by
their proper habits."

• That which completes the rule of decency is
common honesty, by which I understand to mean "the
general received practice of such who, in all other
things, are of a laudable conversation." The apostle
seems to proceed by this rule: "whatsoever things are
comely," or "honest," "whatsoever things are of good
report, think on these things" (Philippians 4:8). Here
he refers to the decision of what is decent to their outward senses.

He refers, first, to their eyes. "Whatsoever things are
comely." So, first, see how well the fashion you wear is
becoming a sober, grave Christian before you put it on.
Consider how a dress sits on the head of a modest,
chaste virgin before you try the experiment yourself.
Second, he refers to their ears: "whatsoever things are
of good report." We should be like that famous artist
who stood close behind his picture to hear what every
man's judgment of it was. Just so should we listen to
what the generality of sober Christians speak and judge
of new modes and fashions. Their censure is enough to
create a suspicion of the appearance of evil, from which
the apostle commands us to abstain (1 Thessalonians

5:22). Again, "provide things honest in the sight of all men," such as carry a conviction of their "comeliness" with them (Romans 12:17). Again, "providing for honest things, not only in the sight of the Lord, but also in the sight of men" (2 Corinthians 8:21). Let the inward garb of your souls, the frame of your hearts, be such as may approve it to God. Let the outward garb and deportment of your bodies be such as may have a good report from good men.

Only here I must recommend to you these cautions:

Caution 1. All customs that authorize and warrant your imitation must be reasonable customs, such as do not clash with nor offend against any maxim of right reason. It is a maxim of reason that the particular modes of apparel should answer the general ends of all apparel; no custom will justify that mode which exposes shame and nakedness to public view. Another maxim of reason is that what was appointed to preserve life should not be perverted to destroy it. It is a maxim of reason that none should glory in that which sin and shame brought into the world, and therefore no apparel should make us proud since all apparel was thus introduced. If an inveterate custom shall plead time out of mind and bolster itself with antiquity, let it know that no custom, however ancient, can prescribe against the law of right reason.

Caution 2. All fashions of apparel that will justify themselves by custom must be able to plead universality among those who in other things make a conscience of their ways and actions. The custom of a few good men, or of many wicked men, will be an unsafe rule by which to judge decency. One speckled bird does not warrant us all to be jays and magpies. Nor should a thousand precedents encourage one sober Christian to herd with those who, in many

other things, give demonstration that they are under
no ties of conscience.

*Caution 3. Not only customs which cross the ends of nature
and the rules of Scripture contribute nothing to the rule of decency, but such as are vain and trifling also.* Our blessed
Savior left us a smart word: "Every idle word that men
shall speak, they shall give account thereof in the day
of judgment" (Matthew 12:36). And if that is true of every idle word, then no doubt it is true of every idle action and practice. A learned paraphrasist renders it that
an idle word signifies "whatever speech is not designed
for some good end and use, neither natural or moral;
discourse that has no tendency to anything that is good
or useful." If that is so, what may we judge of vain apparel, which does not comply with any end of God or
nature, which neither hides, warms, or adorns the
body?

QUESTION 3. From what inward principles are
these outward fashions of apparel taken up?

ANSWER. As is the heart, so is the man; and as is
the man, so commonly will be the garb, the apparel,
and all his outward deportments. An evil mind will give
an evil tincture to everything. "Unto them that are defiled and unbelieving is nothing pure" (Titus 1:15).
Only we must here remember what was observed before:
that though an evil principle will make the action that
proceeds from it sin, a good one will not serve to convert an indifferent action into good if there is not a
concurrence of all other circumstances which ought to
be present. But hence we shall gain one general rule:
all fashions of apparel, however lawful in themselves,
that spring or give indications of an evil heart, are sin-

fully used. Augustus Caesar was wont to say that "rich and gay clothier was either the sign of pride or the nurse of luxury." Perhaps he might be mistaken; nor can any such necessary connection between pride and costly apparel be demonstrated as shall infallibly prove them to be sinful. Nevertheless, when at any time they spring from an evil principle they may, without violating the law of charity, be doomed as evil. It was an argument of the sobriety of Caesar that he never wore any apparel but such as his wife, his sister, or his daughter made for him. Nor indeed do we read of any such trade as that of a tailor in all the Scripture, which argues the simplicity and plainness of their habits, that they needed little art and skill, little labor and pains, to make their clothing.

There are four main principles, among some others, from whence these strange, uncouth fashions may ordinarily arise: levity of mind, vainglory, flattery, and idleness.

Levity of mind is certainly an evil frame, if that may be called a "frame" which never abides so long as to form an acquired habit. Perhaps there is no fashion as foolish as the folly of men, that they will not abide in any. If it was evil, why did you take it up? If it was good, why did you lay it down? It is strange to hear our gallants cry for that fashion today which they will decry and throw away tomorrow, and even more strange to hear a new fashion extolled as the most commodious, convenient, and useful one that ever appeared, and yet, when a newer one starts up, to have the old one decried as absurd, ridiculous, and inconvenient.

Whatever modes of apparel indicate or proceed from a spirit of vainglory are sinfully used. Vainglory is nothing but an inordinate desire for attention. This is when a person is not content with a moderate reputation, such as may vindicate him from contempt and render him serviceable in his station, when he must be either all or nothing. And the malignity of it lies in either hunting after applause for some excellency that the person would be thought to have in him, when he does not have it; in aspiring after glory on the account of some little worth, far more than the thing deserves; or in being ambitious of glory from that which really deserves reproach and contempt.

Hence we have the following rules:

It argues a vicious frame of heart to affect the appearance of being rich by costly apparel when one is really poor. It is no commendable quality to desire to be thought rich. What folly, to be accounted rich when you are poor! What vanity, to desire the shadow when you do not have the substance, or when the shadow eats out the substance. This is the case of too many among us who hang their whole inheritance on their backs, and even that is not yet paid for, but must be set on the backside of the mercer's book.

It argues a proud spirit to affect admiration and applause from clothing. They who have no solid excellency commonly court the notice of the world by some exterior addition of finery.

It argues the most wretched, forlorn spirit that can be imagined to hunt for applause from such fashions as are a shame to your profession, to your person, family, age, sex, and species. If it is sinful to affect glory from beauty, what is it then to affect it from a counterfeit beauty? Tertullian said, "They grievously offend God who daub their skin with ointments and cosmetics, who smear their cheeks with rouge and who blacken their eyebrows. It seems that they are ashamed of God's handiwork. Tertullian also said, in his work *The Female Cult,* "That which is natural is God's own work; and therefore that which is counterfeit and artificial is the invention of the devil."

That apparel which proceeds from or indicates a fawning, adulatory spirit is worn with the sin of the wearer. This was Judah's sin, in her "strange," exotic attire, serviley crouching and accommodating herself to their potent neighbor's fashions that they might insinuate and screw themselves into their favor and affections. Nothing passed for genteel and gallant but what was after the mode of Babylon. This is the disposition of some, whose business it is to lie watching for the first post that may bring them the blessed news in what dress some appeared at the last ball, play, or party.

Some mischiefs have always fatally attended this frenzy. One is that we seldom imitate the modes of apparel of another nation without learning their immoralities, and commonly their idolatries. A second is that the divine justice commonly plagues a people by that nation which they most dote upon. A third is that it is very seldom any nation is fond of the vanities of another without bartering away realities to purchase those vanities; for when lust is clerk of the market, all shall go rather than do without the dearly-beloved vanity.

Whatever fashions or modes of apparel are the result of idleness are justly condemned as sinful. Some seem to have brains whose employment is to do nothing with a world of study. George Herbert noted this well in his poem, "The Church Porch":

> *Much curiousness is a perpetual wooing,*
> *Nothing with labor, folly long a-doing.*

How many misemploy their souls only to undo them! It is as if God had given them immortal spirits capable of serving Him, and they should use them only in contriving how to adorn, but indeed pollute, the body!

QUESTION 4. What are the consequences or affects which these modes and strange fashions of apparel have upon us and others?

ANSWER. Every Christian is bound to consider whether his ways tend, and in what they are likely to issue; not only that his ends and aims are right, but that his actions are such as may reach them. There is the end of the work, and there is the end of the workman. The end of the work is either such as follows necessarily or naturally from it, or else it is that which accidentally or contingently follows thereupon. Thus far we may determine the following:

1. For sober persons to imitate the fashions of the loose so as to take away all external distinction between the virtuous and the debauched is culpable. The apostle would have chastity visible in the conversation, and particularly in the apparel, which is one thing that fills up our conversation (1 Peter 3:2–4). God would not have the world huddled up in a mist, so that all outward differences between the precious and the vile should be taken away. Tertullian is very earnest with sober women who, in their visiting the sick and going to public worship, in all their civil visits and congresses, should apparel themselves so that "there is a visible discrimina-

tion between the servants of God and the handmaids of the devil." It is a pity that there are any such profligate wretches, but seeing that there are and will be so, it is a thousand pities that they should be known by their attire. It was so of old: we read of a young man who was met by a woman with the attire of a harlot; and she was no hypocrite, for her heart was as whorish as her habit (Proverbs 7:10). Judah took Tamar upon suspicion for one of the same character, partly by her veil, but more by her sitting in an open place by the highway side (Genesis 38:14). But we may now take up a lamentation: As is the profane, so is the professor; and as is the harlot, so in this particularly are many whom we hope to be chaste. If a wise man would not willingly be seen abroad in a fool's cloak, why should a modest virgin walk the streets in the garb of the debauched prostitute? Or, if they need to do it, let them not be angry if others judge them as badly as those whom they are ambitious to imitate.

2. That apparel which we find to gratify or awaken corruption in our own souls, though it may be no sin in itself, nor in another to whom it is no such temptation, is a sin for us to wear. We are commanded to "make no provision for the flesh, to fulfill the lusts thereof" (Romans 13:14). In vain do we complain that the fire burns and rages if we pour oil into the flame to feed it; take away the fuel and the fire goes out by itself. If we were true to our own souls, we might find how difficult—if not impossible—it is to wear gorgeous apparel and not be proud of it; to wear gaudy apparel and not feel some vanity awaken within us. The same God who forbids any sin forbids all fomentations of it and all incitements to it. If, then, any apparel or mode of

apparel shall cherish or excite lust in the heart, whatever it is to others, it is sin to him to whom it becomes a provocation. What comfort is it to see another drink a potion without harm when you already feel yourself poisoned by it?

3. Whatever becomes a bait to sin in another ought to be worn with great caution; and the ends of the wearer, and the wear itself, ought to be duly considered. To explain this further, I lay down these propositions:

Proposition 1. To design evil, though the effect does not follow, is sinful. The heart is often criminal when the hand is not or cannot be so. He who hunts for the precious life is a murderer, though God breaks the neck of and defeats the murder. A man may conceive mischief which he cannot bring forth because Providence aborts it. And by this rule, all they are cast who use or abuse lawful apparel for unlawful ends, though they perhaps miscarry in them.

Proposition 2. An evil that is the effect of its proper cause is imputed to him who gave or laid the cause, though he did not actually design the effect. We are responsible to God for all the evil that naturally and necessarily flows from our actions, whatever our designs are or may be. And the reason is because it is supposed that we know, inasmuch as we ought to know, all the natural and necessary moral products of our own actions. This will condemn some of our filthy fashions which of themselves produce these accursed effects. And though God can bring good out of evil, or restrain the evil it might otherwise produce, yet because we cannot, it is evil in us not to prevent it.

Proposition 3. An evil which we ordinarily know has followed, and probably will follow, any action of ours will be

charged on us if we yet adventure upon it. So what if there is
no natural and necessary connection between that evil
and that action? Yet if we see the event to be evil, we are
bound to prevent it if it is in our power. He who knows
the damning power of sin, and what it cost to atone for
it and expiate it—the worth and price of souls, and
what it cost to redeem them—would not be an accidental instrument of the devil to lead into the one or destroy the other by any action of his which he may well
and conveniently refrain.

*Proposition 4. To be an accidental occasion of sin to another
in the remotest order of contingency, though it may not be sin in
us, yet will be some part of our affliction and trouble.* He who
might kill someone accidentally, against his intention,
would be deeply concerned that he might have sent a
soul into eternity, perhaps unprepared.

I will now proceed to examine what directions God
has given to us to walk at a due distance from sinful apparel so that we do not partake of the sin that may be in
them. To these directions I have joined a few considerations to press you to such a cautious walking, and then
I will conclude this discourse.

*Direction 1. Do not be ambitious to appear first in any fash-
ion.* Keep some paces behind those who are zealous to
march in front of a novelty. When the danger is sinning, it is wise to bring up the rear. When custom has
made that which is strange familiar, when time has
mellowed the harshness, and common usage has taken
off the fierce edge of novelty, a good Christian may
safely venture a little nearer, provided he does not leap
over those bounds prescribed by God, nature, and decency. It is time enough to think of following when the

way is well-beaten before us. A modest Christian, in conscience as well as courtesy, will not think it unwise to let others go before him.

Direction 2. Do not strive to come up to the height of fashion. Do not study the criticisms, the niceties, or the punctilios of it. You may be fashionable enough in all conscience without straining to reach the strict exactitude of those superfineries which ill-employed wits have teemed and spawned among us. A general conformity, without forwardness or frowardness, is one branch of that great rule laid down by the apostle: "Let your moderation be known unto all men. The Lord is at hand" (Philippians 4:5). There is a golden median (if we had the skill to hit it) between the peevish singularity of some, who morosely admire obsolete and antiquated garbs, and the precise exactness of others, who make it their religion to depart a hair's breadth from the newest fashions. He who expresses the general usage of the nation without curiosity in the finer strokes and smoother touches of elegance is the man whom I would take and propound to you as a pattern.

Direction 3. Follow no fashion so fast or so far as to run your finances into ruin. Or, as Erasmus said, "Measure yourself by your own foot." Costly apparel is like a prancing steed: he who will follow it too closely may have his brains knocked out for his folly, or rather his empty skull shattered; for the brains have probably gone long before. Advise first with conscience what is lawful, then with your purse what is practical. Consult what you may do, and then what you can do. Some things may be done by others which you may not do; and there are some things which you might lawfully do if you could conveniently do them. All things indifferent are lawful in themselves, but all things are not expedient to some under some circumstances; and what is not expedient, so far as it is not so, is unlawful (1 Corinthians 10:23).

If you will drink from another man's cup, you may be drunk when he is sober; and if you will clothe yourselves at another man's rate, you may be a beggar when he does not feel at all pinched. But how many have run themselves out of their estates into debt, and from the height of gallantry sunk to the depths of poverty, forced either into a jail or out of their country, while they would strain to keep pace with a fashion that was too nimble and fleet for their revenues?

Direction 4. Follow lawful fashions, staying with your equals. But be sure to get right notions of who are your equals. Some may be less than your equals in birth who are more than so in estates; pedigrees and titles will not discharge long bills and reckonings. And some may be your equals in both who are not so in that wherein equity is most valuable. Walk, then, hand-in-hand with those who are heirs together with you of the grace of life (1 Peter 3:7), who are partakers with you of the same precious faith (2 Peter 1:1), who have the same hopes with you of a common salvation (Jude 3). Why should we zealously affect a conformity to them in apparel from whom we must separate in a little time for eternity?

Abraham was a great prince, and yet he dwelt in tents with Isaac and jacob, the heirs with him of the same promise (Hebrews 11:9). And if a tent would serve him and them, why do we make such ado for palaces? Abraham had a promise that he would be "heir of the world" (Romans 4:13), and yet he confessed that he was but a stranger, a pilgrim, a sojourner in the land of promise (Hebrews 11:13), and was always in a traveling garb and habit, ready at a moment's notice to dislodge and follow wherever God should call him. Why then do we dress as if we were at home, citizens of this world, when we are but tenants, and have here no certain dwelling place?

Direction 5. Do not come near those fashions whose numerous implements, trinkets, and tackling require much time in dressing and undressing. No cost of apparel is so ill bestowed as that of precious time in appareling. And if common time is so ill spent, what is the solemn, sacred time laid out in such curiosity! How many sabbaths, sermons, sacraments, prayers, praises, psalms, chapters, and meditations has this one vanity devoured! Let me recommend the counsel of holy Mr. Herbert to you from his poem "The Church Porch":

> *O, be dressed! Stay not for t'other pin!*
> *Why, thou hast lost a joy for it worth worlds!*
> *Thus hell doth jest away thy blessings*
> *And extremely flout thee;*
> *Thy clothes being fast, but thy soul loose about thee!*

Oh, the wanton folly of our times, when it requires no less time to equip and outrig a ship bound for the Indies than a whimsical lady bound for a voyage! With less labor did Adam give names to all the creatures in Paradise than a woman could give you the nomenclature of all the trinkets in her closet. And yet all this is but to consume a whole morning, merely to put on that which will take an entire evening to put off.

Direction 6. Suit your apparel to the day of God's providence, and to the day of His ordinances. God speaks of sackcloth, and are we in our silks and satins? It is incongruous that, when God calls for weeping and mourning, and they who fear His name answer His call, that they should return mirth and jollity, and gorgeous apparel.

By an express law, God granted this privilege to the newly married man, that for 12 months he should be exempt from the wars (Deuteronomy 24:5). And yet, though this indulgence held good when the country was in danger of invasion, no exemption was to be pleaded when the church was exposed to God's indignation. Then "call a solemn assembly; gather the people, sanctify the congregation; let the bridegroom go forth of his chamber, and the bride out of her closet" (Joel 2:15–16). There was no discharge in this war.

But how well was it resented by heaven when, and the denunciation of the divine displeasure against Israel, that God would not go up with them, "the people mourned, and no man did put on him his ornaments" (Exodus 33:3–4).

Direction 7. In all apparel, stay a little above contempt and somewhat more below envy. He who will veer nigh either extreme shall never avoid offense, either for sordidness or superfluity. Do not let your garments smell of either antiquity or novelty. Shun as much an affected gravity as a wanton levity; there may be as much pride in adhering to the antique garbs of our ancestors as there is in courting the modern fooleries. A plain cleanliness is the true medium between sluttishness and gaudiness. Truth commonly lies in the middle between the hot contenders, virtue in the middle between the extreme vices, and decency of apparel in the middle between the height of fashion and merely opposing it. It was only because our corrupt hearts are more prone to the excess than the defect that I laid the rule down, to stay a little more below envy than above contempt.

Direction 8. Let the ornament of the inward man be your rule for adorning the outward man. Take measure of your bodies by your souls, that is, consider well what graces, excellencies, and virtues will adorn a soul; and let something analogical be made the trimming for the body. The apostle will have women "adorn themselves in modest apparel" (1 Timothy 2:9), and especially the graver sort that they be "in behavior as becometh holiness" (Titus 2:3).

OBJECTION. Apparel is not capable of modes or immodesty, of holiness or unholiness!

ANSWER. The garment, or manner of dressing or wearing garments, must be such as indicates and displays such qualities lodging in the soul. Indeed, if we could get the soul suitably adorned, it would cut out, make up, put on, and wear suitable ornaments. The Apostle Peter commands us all to be "clothed with humility" (1 Peter 5:5). Humility is proper wear for a sinner; and if the soul is thus clothed, you may trust it to clothe the body. When the inward man is newly framed and newly fashioned, let it alone to frame and fashion the outward attire. The Platonists say that "it is the soul that forms its house to dwell in."

Direction 9. Get the heart mortified, and that will mortify the clothing. Let grace circumcise the heart, and that will circumcise the long hair and excessive dress, with all the impertinent superfluities that wait on vainglory. Heal the heart of its inward pride and that will retrench the excesses of the outward manifestation. I do not wonder that we find it so difficult to convince women that these gaieties and extravagances of curled hair, painting and patching their faces, are sinful when we cannot convince them of the evil of impenitence and unbelief.

The most compendious way of reforming person, families, nations, and churches is to begin at and deal with the heart; the shortest way to fell a tree is by sound blows at the root. Could we lay the axe to heart-pride, the branches would fall, the leaves would wither, and the fruit would fade, all with one and the same labor. It is an endless labor to demolish this castle of pride by beginning at the top; undermine the foundation, and all the glory of the superstructure falls with it. As a pure, living spring will work itself clean from all the accidental filth that is thrown into it, so cleansing the heart will cleanse the rest. And when the Spirit of Christ undertakes this work—to convince the soul effectually of sin, of the sin of nature and the nature of sin—all these little appendices and appurtenances of vanity will fall and drop by themselves. For this was our blessed Savior's method: "Cleanse the inside of the cup or platter and the outside will be clean also" (Matthew 23:26). And if we could, as only supernatural grace can, "make the tree good," the fruit would be good by consequence (Matthew 12:33).

Direction 10. Whatever fashions of apparel you have found a temptation to your own souls when worn by others, in prudence avoid them. You may reasonably suspect that what has been a snare to you will be a snare to another. For though all are not guilty of the same actual sins, yet all have the same seeds of sin in them; and what has awakened your pride and lust may awaken the same corruptions in your neighbor.

Direction 11. Let all your indifferences be brought under the government and guidance of religion. Indifferent things in their general natures are neither good nor evil; but when religion has the main stroke in managing and ordering them, it will make them good and not evil. Consult with God's glory as to what you should eat, what you should drink, and what you should put on; that will teach us to deny ourselves in some particulars of Christian liberty. "Whether you eat, or drink, or whatsoever ye do, do all to the glory of God" (1 Corinthians 10:31). All the masters of the art of eating, and all the mistresses of the science of dressing, cannot give you a more approved directory than that.

Direction 12. Use all these indifferent things with an indifferent affection for them, an indifferent concern for them and about them. Treat and value them only as they deserve. Clothes do not commend us to God, nor to wise and good men. Why are we then so solicitous about them, as if the kingdom of God lay in them? In considering that the time is short, the apostle would have us "use this world as not abusing it" because "the fashion of this world passeth away" (1 Corinthians 7:29, 31). Yet a little while and there will be no use for clothes because there will be no need for them. But God and the world are commonly of contrary judgments, and "that which is highly esteemed among men" is oftentimes "an abomination in the sight of God" (Luke 16:15). Lukewarmness is a temper hot enough for what is neither good nor evil. How great, then is our sin, who are stone-cold in these matters wherein God would have us "fervent in spirit," but all aflame where He would have us cool and moderate!

Direction 13. Seek that honor chiefly which comes from God alone. The world is never so wise or so good that we should much value its good work or approbation, but is oftentimes so bad and foolish that its commendation is our reproach. What evil have we done that an evil world should speak well of us? To be counted honorable by Him, and made beautiful by Him, is true honor and real beauty. In His judgment stands our absolution or condemnation; in His sentence is our life or death; to Him and by Him we stand or fall (Romans 14:4). What a wretched honor is it that we receive from apparel, which is no part of us, and for which we are beholden to the skill of a tailor or seamstress! But the true reason for the affectation of these vanities lies in that of our Savior: "How can ye believe, which receive honor one of another, and seek not the honor that cometh from God only?" (John 5:44).

And now I close with these considerations, which should press us to such a cautious walking that we do not partake in the sinfulness of strange apparel:

Consideration 1. Seriously consider how apparel came into the world. Sin brought in shame, shame brought in apparel, and apparel has at last brought in more sin and shame. In his state of primitive integrity, man was clothed with original righteousness. He wore the glorious image of Him who created him in knowledge, righteousness, and true holiness (see Colossians 3:10; Ephesians 4:24). But sin has now stripped him of his glory, and exposed his shame to the view of God, his Judge. How great, then, is that pride when we are proud of what should abase us? How vile is that glory that glories in its shame?

It was good advice from Chrysostom: "Let the wearing of our apparel be a perpetual memorial to us of the good things we have lost, and instruction in what penalties mankind is liable to by disobedience." As Gregory Nazianzen reasons: "If we had continued the same as we were at first created, we would have had no need of a coat of skins, the divine image shining in our souls." Therefore Chyrostom's inference is very clear: "Clothes were not given to us to set forth our beauty, but to cover that shame that proceeds from nakedness." And Tertullian excellently prosecutes this argument: "If there was as much faith on earth as there is reward for it in heaven, none of you, since the time you knew God and understood your own condition, who would have affected a joyful, much less a splendid garb; but rather you would have lain in sackcloth and ashes, carrying about the Eve within, lamenting and repenting the scandal of the first sin, and the odium of being the ruin of mankind."

Alas, what pleasure could we take in these vanities if we considered them as the effect of so sad a cause? And what would the gold of Ophir, the pearls of the ocean, or the jewels of the Indies, signify to a soul that was taken up with reflections on its exile from Paradise and the loss of God's image?

Consideration 2. It deserves to be laid to heart how we came into the world, how we must go out, and how we shall rise again. Holy Job confessed that when he was reduced to being a beggar, he was somewhat better than when he was born. "Naked came I out of my mother's womb, and naked shall I return thither" (Job 1:21), that is, to the earth, the common mother of us all. And we may add, "Naked shall I rise again. I shall see my Redeemer at the last day with these eyes, but, I hope, not in these clothes" (see Job 19:25–27). And the apostle said, "We brought nothing into this world, and it is certain that we can carry nothing out" (1 Timothy 6:7). Why then is there all this ado to spruce up a rotten carcass for the short time that we are to tarry here?

We brought nothing in but filth and guilt, and if we carry these out we would have been better off to have never come in. Naked we came here and, if we go from here naked, it would have been better to have stayed behind. To what end, then, is all this waste? All this superfluous cost is but waste. A little will serve nature; less will serve grace; but nothing will satisfy lust. A small matter would serve him who has God for his portion; anything would suffice for this short parenthesis of time were we but well-harnessed out for eternity

Consider, Christians, God has provided "meat for the belly and the belly for meat," clothes for the body and the body for clothes. But God will destroy them all, as for those low ends and uses for which nature or vanity now employs them. Therefore the apostle says, "Having food and raiment, let us therewith be content" (1 Timothy 6:8). Simple food and plain apparel will answer all the demands of nature; and what is more than this is either evil, or else it comes from evil and leads to evil. If it is food, acknowledge God in it, crave His blessing on it, bless Him for it, and glorify Him with it. If it is raiment, God sent it, He indulged it; so own His bounty and bless the Donor. Neither the length of life nor the comfort of life consists in the abundance of what you enjoy (Luke 12:15). And how do you expect to rise again at the last day? It was said affectionately by Tertullian, "I would to God such a miserable sinner as I am might rise up again in the day of the Christian's general triumph to see whether you will rise again with your white, red, and yellow painted faces, with your curls, towers, and wigs; or whether the ministering angels will take up in their arms any painted lady to meet the Lord Jesus Christ in the clouds."

Consideration 3. Let it humble you that God once borrowed man's finest clothing from the beasts. He made them coats of skin (Genesis 3:21). That He clothed them spoke of His mercy; that He clothed them with skins intimated their vileness. Now, have we since then mended the matter, who borrow our choices materials for clothing from the excrement of a worm? If man himself is, as one philosopher said, "the dream of a shadow," and his clothing is but the excrement of a worm, I wonder how he can be proud of it or draw matter of pride from it. A shadow is nothing; a dream of a shadow is something less than nothing—and yet such is man. A worm is vile; but the excrement of a worm is the most vile vileness— and such is all the glory of man in his ruff and pageantry. Nay, man himself is no better. "Man, that is a worm; and the son of man, which is a worm" (Job 25:6). In this verse there are two words rendered "man." One signifies "sickness and misery," the other "earth and dust." And there are two words rendered "worm." One comes from a root that signifies "to lift up the head," and the other signifies "purple and scarlet." This should teach us that man in his best state, when he lifts up his head highest, is but a wretched worm. Some worms are longer, some worms are brighter than others; some, perhaps, may be glowworms. But all are worms, earthworms, clothed by the worms, and at last shall be a feast for worms. Are you proud of your looks? Remember, you are but a worm. Are you proud of your outward shape? Remember, you are still a debtor to the worms; and then be proud if you can. Only know that "man that is in honor, and understandeth not" who made him, why He made him, and who does not answer the ends of his Creator in His creation, "is like the beasts that perish" (Psalm 49:20).

Consideration 4. You have another man, a new man, an inner man, to clothe, adorn, beautify, and maintain. Do not think that you have enough to do to maintain one man well, for you have two. And shall all the care, all the cost, be bestowed on the casing, the cabinet, the shell, while the jewel lies neglected? Think with yourselves, when you are harnessing out for some sumptuous feast, when the jewelry and the garments go on, to conciliate respect in the eyes of others: "Do I have on my wedding garment? Am I ready for the marriage of the Lamb? Do I have on that white garment, so that the 'shame of my nakedness appear not' before a pure and holy God?" (see Revelation 3:18).

Look into the gospel wardrobe. Christ has provided complete apparel to clothe you, as well as complete armor to defend you—and He commands you to put on both. Would you have a chain for your neck which outshines the gold of Peru, or a tiara for your head which shames that of the Persian kings? Then "hear the instruction of thy father, and forsake not the law of thy mother" (Proverbs 1: 8–9) and you have it. Would you have clothing of wrought gold, and wear those robes which "the king's daughter" glories in when she is brought in to the King of glory, so that He may take pleasure in her beauty (Psalm 45:11–13)? Would you wear that jewel "which in the sight of God is of great price," beyond those celebrated ones of Augustus or

Tiberius? Then get "the ornament of a meek and quiet spirit" (1 Peter 3:4). Would you have that which dazzles the diamond and disparages the orient pearl? Then adorn your souls with "modesty, shamefacedness, sobriety, and good works" (1 Timothy 2:9–10).

Would you have the furniture of the gospel? You have it provided by the apostle. First, "put off all these: anger, wrath, malice, blasphemy, lying" (Colossians 3:8; Ephesians 4:25). Anger ferments to wrath; wrath boils up to malice; malice swells up to blasphemy; and all these break out into lying.

Then, "put on, as the elect of God, holy and beloved, bowels of mercies, kindness, humbleness of mind, meekness, longsuffering, forbearing one another, and forgiving one another" (Colossians 3:12–13). And, for an upper garment, "be clothed with humility" (1 Peter 5:5). That your clothes may not sit loose and indecently on you, but stay close and fast, gird yourselves with the girdle of truth (Ephesians 6:14). And would you have all this in one? Then "put on the Lord Jesus Christ" (Romans 13:14). This is the counsel of eloquent Chrysostom: "God looked down from heaven, and saw the whole world naked; not naked as to the body, but destitute of virtue. He saw the sin that they had committed, and He had mercy on them in the transgression they had transgressed. And to these miserable, naked ones He bestowed a garment: Himself."

Here then is your real ornament, your truly gorgeous apparel. In a word, would you have the faithful mirror that will impartially discover all your spots, all your stains, and help you to judge whether they are "the spots of His children" (Deuteronomy 32:5), such as are consistent with the truth and power of godliness, and which will not only reveal them, but wash them away? Then take the glass of God's Word; for therein you view and dress your souls every day. But be sure that you do not forget what manner of person that glass has represented you to your own consciences to be. But "be doers of the Word, and not hearers only, deceiving your own selves" (James 1:22–24).

Consideration 5. Nor let it be forgotten who they were in all ages, recorded for being the most curious and profuse in the mystery of ornaments. We find Jezebel "painting her face and tiring her head," and immediately being eaten by the dogs; only, out of civility or loathing, they left some fragments of her abominable carcass (2 Kings 9:30–37). Among the rest, I would wish her skull were set in a ring, to serve as a death's head to remind our painted ladies of their mortality. The prophet Ezekiel represents the spiritual whoredoms of Judah under the terms of their corporeal luxury: "For whom thou didst wash thyself, paintedst thy eyes, and deckedst thyself with ornaments" (Ezekiel 23:40). That great nothing, Bernice, had such a stock of impudence that she dared face a court of judicature, and "came with abundance of pomp and fantastical bravery" (Acts 25:23).

We must not forget that great strumpet Cleopatra, who wore a pearl worth £50,000, which in a prodigal frolic she dissolved in vinegar, and in a glass of wine drank in one draught. And it might cool the fervor of our ladies when they read of "a woman arrayed in purple and scarlet color, and decked with gold and precious stones and pearls," and then hear that she was "the mother of harlots" (Revelation 17:3–5). And when Platina, the Romanists' own historian, informs us that Pope Paul II painted his face (a shame in a woman, a greater shame in a man, and greater still in him who would be called "the head of the catholic church"), I hope they will not condemn the Protestants of incivility if they now and then call his successors "the whore of Babylon." St. Jerome tells us that Maximilla, the pretended prophetess, but really the whore of Monitanus, painted her eyes with stibium. And history rings with the effeminate luxury of the monster of men, Heliogabalus, who never wore one suit twice, and studded his shoes with pearls and diamonds. Poppaea, the infamous wife of execrable Nero, had the bridles and all the furniture of her mules made of pure gold, and with the same metal, or at least silver, they were shod. But let these patters not provoke your imitation, but stir up your indignation.

Consideration 6. How heinous is it that sin of endeavoring to procure the acceptance of men by that which is an abomination to God! Must it not highly provoke His majesty, to see the critics of artificial beauty put out God's work in a second edition, as if it had been incomplete as it came first out of God's hands! Yet such is the operose study of our fashion experts: what nature made black, they will make white; what age has made white, they will make black. Time has left them bald, but by false hair they will restore youth.

St. Jerome said, "Here is a lady who paints her face and, to the reproach of her Creator, would appear fairer in the eyes of men than ever nature made her." How displeasing is it to God to be displeased with what He has done, that they may please the worst of men!

It is objected by those who paint their faces that they are good women, and do it only to please their husbands, so that they may keep a place in their affections, since they are now grown old and are not so attractive as in their youthful and florid days. And they think they have a clear text that justifies their pious intentions. 1 Corinthians 7:34: "She that is married careth for the things of the world, how she may please her husband."

To this I give the same answer as did Peter Martyr: "Let them do so with all their heart; let them strive to please their husbands. But be sure that they do not cheat and abuse him while they please him. For let them make it their own case: would they be so duped as to marry a deformed, ugly fellow, whom they took to be a handsome and beautiful person?" Chrysostom said, "An understanding man would see his wife's face as God made it. And once women have taught their husbands to be in love with painted faces, they will rather send them to professed whores than tie them closer to themselves; because common harlots are a thousand times more expert in these adulterations than honest women."

And if it is a sin to sophisticate and adulterate wares and merchandise, how much more to paint the face! Augustine said, "For a woman to paint her face so that she may appear either more fair or more ruddy is an adulterating fallacy; and, I am confident, husbands would not willingly have such a trick put upon them."

To conclude, if the husband is a wicked man, he will suspect his wife's honesty all the more, and be tempted to return like for like. If he is a good man, he will need none of these artificial means to secure his affections, but out of conscience will acquiesce in his own choice, and the law and will of God.

Consideration 7. Seriously weigh what a long train of sins waits upon the stately lady of vainglory. Pride never walks the streets alone, nor without a vast retinue of lusts to adorn her pageantry. He who will be profuse in one instance must be covetous in another; riotous spending is accompanied with penurious sparing. A great fire must have a great store of fuel to feed it; and an open table requires an abundance of provision to maintain it. Pride must be maintained by oppression, fraud, and deceit. If the tradesman's wife overspends in the streets, the husband must make it up one way or another in the shop; they who spend unmercifully must gain unconscionably. The mill will not grind unless some lust brings gist to it.

Nor it is one single sin that fills the train of pride. God is robbed of His worship, the poor of their charity, the creditor of his just debts, and posterity of those portions which parents are bound to lay up for their children. Pride drinks the tears of widows and orphans, revels in the hard labors of the indigent, and feeds on the flesh of thousands. Elegantly did Tertullian say, "A vast estate is enclosed in one small locket. A necklace worth almost £8,000 hangs on one single string; a slender neck carries lordships and manors; and the thin tip of the ear wears a jewel or pendant that would defray the charges of housekeeping for a year." This is the evil of what the apostle called "costly apparel" in 1 Timothy 2:9.

Consideration 8. How many precious souls has this one vanity destroyed or endangered with superfluous apparel! How often has your own clothing been your own temptation, as the proud horse is made more proud with his bells and trappings. Is it not enough that we have a devil to tempt us; but we must be so to ourselves? How often has apparel drawn out the seeds of corruption which otherwise would have laid under the dirt and never sprouted! How often has it blown up the sparks of concupiscence which otherwise would have laid buried under the ashes! Is not Satan malicious and subtle enough without us doing his work for him, or rendering it more feasible?

And how you endanger the souls of others! Wicked men are hardened in their pride by your example. They triumph in you as their converts and proselytes; they glory that the professing Christian has now become one of them. Others are tempted to think that all religion is false when it cannot prevail with those who profess it to deny one vanity, when that religion itself teaches them to deny all! Who can expect that a man should deny his profit and gain who cannot deny an inexpensive and chargeable foolery? Or how will that man deny himself in the bulk when he cannot refuse the blandishment of so small a branch of it? How many poor, innocent souls, perhaps a little inclined to entertain better thoughts of religion, have been seduced to unchaste thoughts, designs, and actions! Now, how many may be in hell whom your bewitching, whorish attire has first drawn into sin, and then sent down to hell! Do not say (if you are a Christian you will not say it), "I will use my liberty and wear what I judge convenient; if others take offense and stumble, it is their sin, not mine. If they took offense, I gave them no cause; and therefore let them be damned at their own peril." But if you knew—or seriously considered what you knew—the price of a soul's redemption, you would not hazard its damnation. Silver and gold may damn a soul, but cannot ransom or recover one. What a cut it would be to your heart if you could lay your ear to the gates of hell, and hear the roarings, cursings, and blasphemies of that miserable lot; how they blaspheme divine justice, curse themselves and, among others, you, who were an occasion to send them there with your tempting bravery! Hear Tertullian: "Why, then, do you provoke lust in your own heart? Why do we endanger the souls of others? He who presumes, fears little, uses little precaution, and runs into great danger. Fear is the origin of security, but presumption is the enemy of fear."

I easily grant that there is a great difference between a cause and an occasion of evil. A cause is much more than an occasion; yet the latter is not so small and light a matter but that many of God's weighty laws were grounded on this, so that the occasion of sin in themselves and others might be avoided. The civil law determines that if archers shooting at targets kill a man passing by on the road, they must make satisfaction. If a man falls into a pit built to catch wild beasts, those who built it will be punished; and he shall be severely punished who, sent to watch a furnace, falls asleep and lets a fire arise that burns down the house. But the New Testament is very full: we are not to lay a stumbling block nor an occasion of offense, nor to use our liberty in that wherein our weak brother is offended (Romans 14:13, 21).

Consideration 9. Pride is the forerunner of destruction, whether personal, domestic, or national. "Pride goeth before destruction, and a haughty spirit before a fall" (Proverbs 16:18). This truth was so obvious to the heathens that Seneca could say:

The morn beheld him vain and proud;
The night, enveloped in his shroud!

There is the pride of the rich who "boast themselves in the multitude of their riches" (Psalm 49:6). There is the pride of the ambitious, who swell with titles and dignities; and there is the childish pride of women and effeminate men, who glory in apparel. And though this last may seem below the notice of divine vengeance, yet these light and small things draw down great and heavy judgments. Isaiah 3:18–23 speaks of trifling and ludicrous things, such as "tinkling ornaments, round tires like the moon," and "nose jewels," very uncomely in such Epicurean swine. And though many of them seem to be innocent, such as "bonnets, earrings, and mantles," yet God threatens that "instead of a sweet smell there shall be a stink; and instead of a girdle, a rent; and instead of well-set hair, baldness; and instead of a stomacher, a girding of sackcloth; and burning instead of beauty." All these threatenings were accomplished in the Babylonian captivity, where God sent them to spare the cost and trouble of fetching home their new fashions, their strange apparel.

Archbishop [James] Ussher and Mr. [Robert] Bolton, two great lights of our church, have long since forewarned us that God would punish us by that nation which we were so ambitious to imitate in their fashions of apparel. And how much is the ground of fear increased since their days! The plague is never more easily conveyed than in clothes; and it is to be feared that, with their strange, apish fashions, we have imported their vicious manners, if not their idolatries. The degeneracy of the Romans in this point prognosticated their declining greatness; and there is no more easy observation than that, when a people cease to be great in generous and noble achievements, they begin to affect this trim way of glory by apparel.

The use and application will be your own. This sermon will never be complete till you have preached it to your souls by meditation, and to the world by a thorough reformation. And if you slight this advice and counsel, remember the text, that God "in the day of His sacrifice, will punish all such as are clothed with strange apparel."